decorative hardware

INTERIOR DESIGNING
WITH KNOBS, HANDLES,
LATCHES, LOCKS, HINGES,
AND OTHER HARDWARE

liz gordon
and terri hartman
of liz's antique hardware

photography by
philip clayton-thompson

ReganBooks
An Imprint of HarperCollinsPublishers

HarperCollins books may be purchased for educational, business, or sales
promotional use. For information please write: Special Markets Department,
HarperCollins Publishers Inc., 10 East 53rd Street, New York, NY 10022.

FIRST EDITION

Designed by Joel Avirom and Jason Snyder

Printed on acid-free paper

Library of Congress Cataloging-in-Publication Data has been applied for.

ISBN 0-06-039289-4

00 01 02 03 04 TP 10 9 8 7 6 5 4 3 2 1

*To Peter, without whom
there never would have been
a Liz's Antique Hardware.*

— LG

To Doc.

— TH

acknowledgments

We would sincerely like to thank:

The present and past staff of Liz's Antique Hardware, who are responsible for our daily successes and enabled us to make a dream come true;

Ilvio Gallo, for his artistic vision and expertise;

Doc Farnsworth, for his invincible optimism, unfailing good humor, and unending labor;

Philip Clayton-Thompson, for his beautiful photographs and sly wit;

Donna Pizzi, for her unequaled styling and wisdom;

Our hardware suppliers, for their creativity and resourcefulness;

The Antique Doorknob Collectors of America, for their undying passion about the study of builders' hardware;

And our families, for a lifetime of encouragement, especially Rose Gordon-Greenberg, who initially made it all possible, and Jane Werhane, who shared her son so graciously.

vii

contents

part I:
styles through time

part II: inspirations,
options, answers

preface

More than twenty years ago I found myself in another dealer's beautifully chaotic warehouse, inspecting the merchandise he wanted to liquidate. Chairs and tables hung from the rafters, and staircase balustrades, fireplace mantels, and household remnants were piled in the center of the room. Small glistening objects spilled from the barrels stacked on their sides seven high against the walls. Looking closely, I noticed that these objects were doorknobs, something I saw every day of my life, but felt as if I were seeing for the first time. These weren't the doorknobs I knew. They were far more beautiful than any I had ever seen. At that moment, with the brass and glass knobs catching the sunlight streaming through the warehouse windows, I saw my future.

So I purchased all that merchandise and set up shop in that same warehouse. I initially sold general antiques, but I constantly found myself drawn to the hardware. It fascinated me, and I learned as much as I could about it. My course of study was quite practical; at that time there were no books or articles about hardware, so all the buildings I found myself in and all the pieces of furniture I saw became my textbooks. Eventually I began to specialize in hardware.

Six years later I decided to move to San Diego. It wasn't feasible to pack up my whole warehouse, but it was feasible to pack up my inventory of hardware. So fifty 50-gallon drums of hardware—

doorknobs, doorplates, hinges, locks, furniture hardware—and I followed the sun. My business made the official change from Liz's Antique Warehouse into Liz's Antique Hardware.

After seven years in San Diego it was time for another change, and I headed to Los Angeles. I found a terrific building—a former dry cleaner's—on La Brea Avenue, which in the early 1990s was just beginning a transformation from a somewhat forlorn strip of small retail stores into a collection of design and lifestyle-oriented shops.

Then my customers found me. The timing of my move couldn't have been better. Los Angeles is full of homes built in the early decades of the twentieth century, and in the early 1990s a wave of young home owners began restoring and renovating those residences. We could provide the hardware and lighting those older homes needed.

And our customers provided a lot of support and enthusiasm. Some home owners returned week after week, meticulously sorting through hinges to find ten matching pairs or gazing one more time at the huge 1920s wrought-iron chandelier decorated with graceful dragons. In the early days, it was the repeat customers—the ones who walked through the door, smiled knowingly at the salesperson, and, without saying a word, walked straight to the milk crate of glass knobs—who really made it worthwhile. Sure, they kept the store financially viable, but they also shared our love of decorative hardware, and they proved that such an unusual endeavor could work.

I continued to scour the country on buying trips, but it became harder and harder to supply the store with as much antique hardware as the customers needed. If someone wanted thirty-five matching cabinet knobs for their kitchen, we were hard-pressed to help them. Fate intervened again. The catering company next door went out of business and we took over the space, opening The Hardware Gallery, where we feature contemporary and reproduction hardware and lighting.

Over the years, excited by the possibilities that arise from a trip to the store, customers have asked the staff to recommend a good general information book about decorative hardware. There just aren't any, a fact that has been gnawing at me for years as I've tried to do my own research. There are technical treatises and price guides, which certainly fill a need, but there aren't any beautifully photographed books about hardware and its role in the American decorative arts.

So Terri Hartman and I decided to write our own book. It was time, we decided, to answer the questions our customers—and we ourselves—have asked over the years. We also want to share our excitement about hardware. We sincerely hope that this book will not only answer your questions, but also leave you with a new appreciation for decorative hardware and its functional beauty.

—*Liz Gordon*

introduction

At the beginning of the twentieth century the centerpiece of a well-to-do American parlor was the Tiffany lamp. The crowning achievement of the decorative arts, this beautiful object reigned as the focal point amid the potted palms, overstuffed chairs, and assorted bric-a-brac. And befitting its exalted status, it came with its own unspoken admonishment: "Do not touch. My beauty is fragile. Turn me on if you must—but gently. And if you need more light, sit closer to the fire."

In that same room were decorative objects that embodied the identical forces of current style, used the same quality of materials, and aspired to the same level of design excellence as the Tiffany lamp. But despite their inherent beauty, they went almost unnoticed. But certainly not untouched. For these were knobs, handles, latches, locks, and hinges. They were the workhorses of the decorative arts. Designed to be used repeatedly through generations, decorative hardware was unsung, unappreciated, and absolutely indispensable.

In a hundred years very little has changed. Open. Close. Latch. Lock. These actions in many ways define the functional aspects of decorative hardware. This is what decorative hardware does. Without it much of our world would simply cease to function. Drawers wouldn't open, windows wouldn't close, and doors wouldn't lock. Decorative hardware gives motion to our world. It is the interface between us and much of the physical world we live in.

But function is only part of what makes decorative hardware such an invaluable part of our lives. Because these most humble of functional objects are so integral to our lives, they act as key building blocks of decorative style. Whether used to stylistically accent a piece or to stylistically join together many different facets, decorative hardware, by its very ubiquitous nature (always there, always close at hand, always right in front of our eyes), is always going to make a statement of style.

The irony of course is that because we are surrounded by decorative hardware we take it for granted, and it becomes invisible to us. But the reality is that not only does the proper knob make a door function, it helps create a unified stylistic statement. With the wrong type of knob, the door may not open. With the wrong style of knob, the door may open, but it will not work decoratively. The right hardware creates harmony between function and style.

Because it sits right at the intersection between design and function, decorative hardware is a wonderful window into the history of both architecture and the decorative arts in America. Each piece of hardware gives us an insight into all the forces at work when it was designed and manufactured. Therefore hardware becomes the perfect way to examine the various decorative styles that have evolved through the history of American design.

You'll notice that we make a distinction between styles and periods. Periods refer to blocks of time. Within each period, many different decorative styles may coexist. Having said that, we have to point out the exception that proves the rule: the adjective "Victorian" can be used to describe both a period and a style.

In Part I we look at the history of decorative hardware in America, examining its two main components: building hardware, used on doors and windows, and furniture hardware, used on freestanding pieces of furniture and on built-in cabinets.

The story of American decorative hardware is filled with struggles between divergent forces—between function and style, domestic pride and foreign influence, the elite and the masses, rural life and urban life, and the comforts of the past and the promise of the future.

It is a story that begins simply enough at the anvil and forge of the village blacksmith. Prior to the Industrial Revolution, American decorative hardware was made primarily from iron. It was heavy in form and function and light on style.

What style it did have came from England. This importation of English style would become a key element of American decorative hardware and would continue for the next one hundred and fifty years. It would also lead to a great irony.

The first mass-produced style of hardware in America would be named after an Englishman—and, in fact, one who detested the very thought of mass production. Charles Eastlake, much to his chagrin, gave his name to a type of American hardware that became popular here in the late 1860s and was known for its elaborate, stylized geometric forms. Eastlake style hardware was a three-dimensional representation of the nation's relief at the conclusion of the Civil War and its exuberance with its new industrial muscle.

The next significant style of American design, Victorian, was rampant in its excess. Here in the United States, Victorian style hardware was available in a profusion of choices. Although these choices were made possible by the Industrial Revolution, they were styled to provide comfort in a troubling time, using design elements that harkened backward and employing themes from the past.

Consumers began to look to the decorative arts as a source of solace in a world turned upside down in just a few short years. In the face of the unrelenting pressures of a newly industrialized world, designers would repeatedly return to the past for themes— just as America would return to England for design inspiration.

The next significant decorative style to sweep America was born in just such a manner. From the late 1800s to the early 1920s, American designers used the "hand-crafted" philosophical ideals of the British Arts and Crafts movement to create a style of decorative arts. Ultimately, however, the style was handmade in appearance only. The Arts and Crafts style hardware decorating new suburban bungalows across the nation was mass-produced, and special metal finishes were used to make the hardware appear handwrought.

While the Arts and Crafts style was based on a philosophical model, the Revival styles in America, prevalent from the turn of the century until the Second World War, were based on romantic historical references. Somewhat incongruously, Tudor Revival homes and Spanish Colonial Revival homes proudly stood side by side as Americans created safe worlds in burgeoning suburbs across the land. Decorative hardware was doing its part to make every home a castle.

While the majority of Americans were snug in their Revival homes, a new movement was brewing in Europe. As it spread to America, this movement would change two ingrained patterns of American design. Art Deco was the first American decorative style that had its genesis in France, not in England, and it was also the first American decorative style that looked to the future instead of the past. Never a style of the masses, from the mid-1920s through the mid-1940s Art Deco and its later incarnation, Streamline Moderne, brought an elegant, curvaceous, and sensuous feeling to American decorative design.

Art Deco conveyed confidence, an emotion that would die during the Great Depression and the Second World War. But when the war ended, confidence returned, and Moderne became modern. For the first time, America created its own look. Mixing clean lines with a stark functionalism and refuting any historical embellishments, Mid-Century Contemporary style decorative hardware epitomized the can-do, no-nonsense spirit of the times.

When the American decorative hardware industry was born, fewer than one hundred and fifty years ago, it took twenty years for a style to cross the Atlantic. Now it can take seconds. Here, where the Industrial Age coexists with the Digital Age, today's style is tomorrow's revival. We live in the stylistic age of "anything goes." No one style dominates.

using decorative hardware

Because so many styles are available to consumers, the opportunities for using hardware to fulfill a personal design vision are limitless. If you live in an authentic historic restoration, or if you're restoring an authentic piece of furniture, the information in the chapters on historic styles will tell you which style of hardware your home or furniture needs. But if you don't live in a historic home (and face it, most of us don't), you can still use decorative hardware to create your own style. There are many ways of incorporating both antique and contemporary hardware into personal decorating styles—the details provided by doorknobs and cabinet handles can become the decorative springboard for rooms throughout the home.

That's why Part II illustrates how to use decorative hardware in innovative ways, presenting a room-by-room tour highlighting some creative, exciting, contemporary uses. In living rooms and dining rooms, decorative hardware takes a formal turn, presenting your home, your style, to your guests. Hardware in family rooms becomes a bit less restrained, and in the bedroom—your refuge—you can use hardware to express yourself any way you want. Kitchens and bathrooms provide the most innovative contemporary uses of decorative hardware. From a completely new bathroom designed to look one hundred years old to a comfortable family kitchen using a mixture of materials and textures, you'll see a wealth of ideas on incorporating antique, contemporary, and reproduction hardware.

You'll also discover where to find hardware, from down-and-dirty salvage yards to upscale specialty stores. You'll see what to look for when shopping for hardware: how to tell if you've found the right piece for a particular door, window, or piece of furniture and how to determine that piece's quality. Five completely different styles of drawer pulls in one family kitchen will illustrate the transformative powers of hardware. Finally, you'll learn the basic methods of cleaning hardware and see how to replace a modern doorknob with an antique one.

By the time you've finished this book, we hope you'll have a new appreciation for hardware, the most tactile of the decorative arts. Hopefully, you'll understand both its history and its potential so that the next time you turn a doorknob, you'll pause just a second to marvel at its functional beauty.

part I:
styles
through
time

early american style hardware

1607 to 1865

Prior to the Industrial Revolution, American hardware was usually handmade. The emphasis was on function over style. And most of the style—as well as some of the materials—was imported from England. Innovations during the period included mortise locks, the first uniquely American style of furniture and furniture hardware, and the first American hardware factories. Hardware of the time was simple, plain, heavy, and functional.

3

The first Europeans to settle in America were far more concerned with subsistence than with style. Their first buildings were plain, unornamented versions of the homes they left across the ocean.

Local building materials and climate determined the basic shape of these early houses. In the Northeast, British settlers built simple, one or one-and-a-half story wooden homes with steeply pitched roofs and huge central chimneys. In the Mid-Atlantic, brick houses had end chimneys. Both styles featured casement windows with small, leaded, diamond-shaped paned windows that opened inward or outward. In the Southwest, the thick adobe walls of the homes built by Spanish settlers provided insulation against the cold in the winter and the heat in the summer. The very simple iron hardware used in all these homes was usually made by a local blacksmith with an eye toward function, not style.

Iron thumb latches were one of the earliest types of door hardware used in America. They were used on both interior and exterior doors.

finding it

Because it's more than two hundred years old, not much original Early American hardware still exists. What does exist is concentrated in New England and along the East Coast.

There are some very good reproduction sources for Early American iron hardware. Also, some contemporary companies make very simple, substantial brass knobs like those imported from Britain in the seventeenth and eighteenth centuries.

practical considerations

Strap hinges are the easiest type of Early American hardware to find. Be careful, though, because the pintle—the pin upon which the two halves pivot—is often missing. If this is the case, an ironworker can make a replacement pintle.

Early American iron hardware may be quite rusty. If the rust is on the surface, it can be easily cleaned with WD-40 and steel wool. If the rust has eaten through the iron, the hardware is unusable.

If you're using thumb latches, check with your local building department to make sure the latches meet your area's building codes.

decorative considerations

Iron strap hinges and thumb latches add a touch of authenticity to rustic homes.

Thumb latches would be particularly appropriate in less ornate Revival style homes, but would look ridiculous in a 1915 Victorian or a 1955 modernist glass house.

5
·
early
american
style hardware

above right: Shutter stays or "dogs" hold shutters open. The simple S shape is the most common shutter dog.

right: The inside of a door using a thumb latch. When the thumb piece on the exterior of the door is depressed, the horizontal bar lifts, disengaging from the keeper on the jamb and enabling the door to open.

opposite: Heavy iron strap hinges accompanied thumb latches.

A stay is a very rudimentary cabinet latch; a piece
of wood is screwed into the surface of one door and
the overlapping tongue keeps the other door shut.

left: In a dining room, the brass knobs and turn latches on the 1823 Lehigh County pine corner cupboard are original.

right: The pine pewter chest was made in Montgomery County, Pennsylvania, in 1754. The brass Chippendale handles were either imported from England or made illegally in America.

In the early 1700s the British colonies spread out along the Atlantic seaboard. As towns developed and the settlers became more comfortable in the New World, building styles became more sophisticated.

Built for permanence, early-eighteenth-century homes were two stories, with symmetrical front façades and gable roofs. As glass became cheaper, double-hung sash windows, with one or both sashes moving up or down, replaced the small diamond-shaped paned casement windows.

Northern cities like Boston, Philadelphia, and New York developed their own urban housing type: row houses. Built in a row along a street, a group of row houses shares side walls for structural support.

In a typical eighteenth-century urban home, large ornamental exterior door hinges signified the substance of the door and, by extension, the substance of the home owner. The exterior and interior door hardware consisted of either locally made iron latches and knobs or sparkling brass knobs imported from Britain.

Early colonists were allowed to use British brass hardware only. The Navigation Acts and Acts of Trade passed by Parliament between 1660 and 1696 outlawed brass foundries in the colonies. Designed to protect Britain's flourishing hardware industry, centered in Birmingham, these laws stipulated that certain goods, like brass hardware, could be purchased only from the mother country.

After the Revolutionary War, American brass founders began selling their own hardware. It was heavy and very plain, emphasizing function rather than ornament. It wasn't until the 1830s, when the first American hardware factories were established in Connecticut,

left: The gleaming mahogany veneer Empire style dresser with wooden knobs was made around 1840.

right: The knob captures the beautiful grain of the mahogany.

9
early american style hardware

left: Simple as it seems, this kitchen is as it was in the home of a prosperous shipping magnate of the 1860s. Because the lady of the house rarely set foot in the kitchen, most kitchens were designed for work, not for style.

right: This distinctive bin pull, known as a "doggie" pull, was patented in 1870 by the Metallic Compression Casting Company of Boston. It was one of the first mass-produced pieces of hardware.

that American manufacturers began to mass-produce and to experiment on a large scale with other materials in addition to brass and iron. Regional artisans had always used locally available materials—like glass, wood, pottery, and porcelain—for doorknobs, and in the early nineteenth century these same materials were used for mass-produced work.

In building hardware, the major technological development of the period was the mortise lock. Up until this time, both exterior and interior door locks used rim-locks, which were surface-mounted on the door. A small knob or stirrup-shaped ring on the outside of the door operated the lock.

The mortise lock, a British innovation, fits into a recess carved in the door instead of sitting on the face of the door. The dominant form of lock for the next hundred years, mortise locks are still used today.

above: Mid-nineteenth-century sophistication: the mahogany dresser in a well-to-do woman's bedroom features Sandwich glass knobs. These cut-glass knobs were first produced in the late 1820s in Sandwich, Massachusetts. Later knobs in the same style that weren't made in Massachusetts are also known as Sandwich glass.

opposite: The radiance of the curtain tieback and doorknob comes from mercury glass, which was first produced in America around 1850. Mercury glass gets its name from the manufacturing process, in which a silver nitrate solution is adhered to the inside of the glass. The glass appears silvery and shiny, like mercury. Dating from the same period, the side table is in the Federal style, with simple pressed brass knobs.

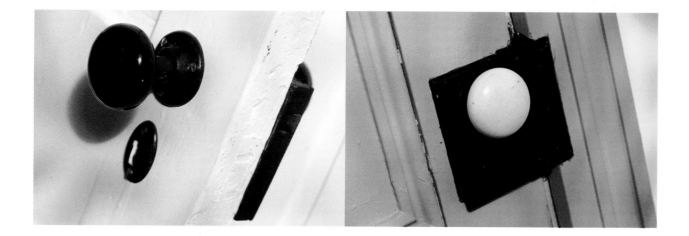

Throughout this early period until the late 1800s, when built-in cabinetry became popular, the hardware used on fine American furniture was more elegant and decorative than the building hardware of the same period. On freestanding furniture the hardware needed to harmonize with the piece of furniture, not with the overall aesthetic of the building.

Early American furniture makers copied their British colleagues, creating tables, chests, and desks in styles like William and Mary, Queen Anne, and Chippendale. The hardware for this furniture was usually imported from Britain; if the hardware was made in the United States, it was a replication of British styles. There was no original style of American furniture hardware during this period; the finer hardware was either English or based on English designs, and the more rudimentary hardware consisted of simple wooden or iron knobs and stays.

On the whole, American hardware in the early decades of the 1800s wasn't much different than it was in the early 1600s. Simplicity of design was dictated by complexities of manufacturing. Function—not style—dominated hardware design during this period. With the coming of the Industrial Revolution to America, the country itself would change in previously unimaginable ways. And hardware styles would be a bellwether of that change.

eastlake style hardware

The Industrial Revolution transformed every aspect of American life, and hardware was no exception. Choices of styles and materials exploded. As in the past, the primary design influences were imported. But even though one of the first mass-produced American design styles was named for an Englishman, it was, as far as that Englishman was concerned at least, infuriatingly American.

Innovations during the period include mass-produced and mass-marketed hardware, building and furniture hardware with a single stylistic theme, the founding of American hardware's "big three"—Russell and Erwin, P. & F. Corbin, and Yale and Towne—and the birth of suburbia. The hardware was elaborate, stylized, extravagant, and incised.

15
▪

While original to the house, this Eastlake doorknob and doorplate combination is unusual: although the plate and knob are in the same pattern, the knob is brass and the plate is iron. Usually the metals were not mixed; in fact, in most cases the metal used for door hardware indicated the importance of the room. On the first floor, decorative brass hardware was used. The family's rooms on the second floor used decorative iron hardware, and often the hardware in the servants' quarters was completely undecorated.

American Eastlake hardware is based on an irony. The "Eastlake" style of architecture and decorative arts was named for a man who abhorred everything about the style. Charles Locke Eastlake, an English architect, furniture designer, and critic, wrote a manual on interior decoration entitled *Hints on Household Taste in Furniture, Upholstery, and Other Details.* Published in London in 1868 and in Boston in 1872, the book was a gigantic success, with seven American editions by 1883. Unfortunately for Mr. Eastlake, his American readers weren't looking for a message, they were looking at the pictures.

Chock-full of furniture, this Eastlake entrance hall, with its richly carved walnut staircase and fireplace mantel, is the epitome of the style.

opposite: The doorknob and plate echo the elaborate detailing of the period.

right: Eastlake door hinges were also decorative, and usually the same decorative pattern was used for all the hardware in the house. When the hinge-pin finials are pointed, the hinge is referred to as "steeple-tipped" and when the finials are round, the hinge is known as "ball-tipped." This hinge is brass with a nickel plating, and even the steeple-tip finials are decorated. The background of the design was always blackened to bring out the incised detailing.

Many things were lost in the translation when Americans read *Hints on Household Taste.* Lost was Eastlake's dissatisfaction with the vast social changes wrought in England by the Industrial Revolution. Lost was his plea for a return to a simpler, more handmade aesthetic. Lost was his battle against the decorative excesses of Victorian England.

American readers just didn't get the point. Eastlake was reacting to events in England that had not yet transpired in the United States. Twenty years behind the Industrial Revolution curve, America was just beginning to flex its industrial muscle. We hadn't become excessive . . . yet.

using eastlake hardware

finding it

There's quite a bit of original Eastlake hardware still available. It can be found all over the country, but the best selection is in the Midwest, where the first wave of suburban expansion took place in the last decades of the nineteenth century.

A few companies reproduce Eastlake hardware. These reproductions run the quality gamut from relatively inexpensive pressed-metal pieces to fine, museum-quality cast pieces. The prices of these pieces run the same gamut.

Eastlake hardware is being reproduced in only the most common patterns, not in every pattern originally manufactured.

practical considerations

The biggest challenge in using original Eastlake hardware will be finding the quantity of pieces you need. Eastlake hardware was manufactured in dozens of different patterns, so if you want all the door

and window hardware in your home to match, it will take a bit of time and patience.

If you're intent on restoring your home with hardware to match what was originally intact, consider using a mixture of original and reproduction hardware (if your pattern is being reproduced).

Eastlake hardware was manufactured before there was standard sizing in the hardware industry. Not all knobs fit all plates. Nor does every double-hung window latch fit every window catch. Carry samples when shopping so you can be sure of a perfect fit.

A very big problem with retrofitting doors that have been cut for contemporary cylindrical lock-sets with Eastlake hardware is that Eastlake interior doorplates and rosettes are—without exception—too narrow to cover the existing hole.

decorative considerations

With its strong detailing, Eastlake hardware can become a decorative accent in almost any style of room. It works very well in Victorian settings, and the more geometric Eastlake patterns are very fitting for Art Deco interiors. Asian-inspired rooms are also great backgrounds for Eastlake hardware. Arts and Crafts and Revival style interiors, with their handmade, "rough-hewn" emphasis, would not be a good match for the stylized sophistication of Eastlake hardware.

Eastlake was reacting to very real forces in England. As manufacturing processes industrialized, the green agricultural countryside gave way to rows of malodorous brick factories. The trained artisans who made up a good portion of the middle class disappeared. In their place arose two new classes, wealthy industrial owners and untrained factory workers. England's economic and social order, which had existed virtually unchanged for centuries, was completely transformed by a redistribution of wealth and power within several decades.

right: Another study in abundance. Pocket doors lead from the parlor into the sitting room. So-called because they slide into the wall, pocket doors enabled several smaller rooms to combine into a single large room for social functions. In the days before central heating, it was also useful to be able to close off rooms for heat conservation.

opposite: When a pocket door is completely open, all the hardware recesses into the wall and disappears, except for the plate on the edge of the door. To close the door, you push the button on the edge of the door and the pull pops out. You can then pull the door closed.

The decorative arts were affected by the changes in the means of
the production and the social order. Decorative objects like vases
and plant stands were expensive when produced by hand, but were
inexpensive when made by machines. Once the proud possessions
of only the very rich, these pieces now proclaimed their middle-class
owners' social aspirations. In an era when affluence became more
accessible, the trappings of affluence became more visible. English
Victorian interiors were cluttered with groupings of bowls, vases,
figurines, photographs, and paintings. Style reigned over function.

The brass-plated cast-iron
pushplate on a swinging
door between pantry and
dining room makes its
intentions clear.

In the sitting room, a movable feast—all the furniture is on casters.

Eastlake and his fellow reformers decried this excess. They felt that interiors should be simple and even somewhat restrained. Furniture should not display the curving forms of the Rococo Revival style then popular in England, but instead should be simple and handmade of solid wood with joined and "honest" (visible) construction. Ornament should always be related to function. The pieces illustrated in his book are quite simple, with little decoration beyond scalloped moldings and decorative carvings.

Eastlake's writing was ignored, but his drawings were widely copied. English and American manufacturers of inexpensive, machine-made furniture (the very furniture he was denouncing) reproduced his furniture, using machine-made moldings in place of his hand-turned details and applying extraneous surface decoration wherever possible.

Eastlake was aghast at this development, and at the use of his name. In the fourth London edition of his book he wrote, "I find American tradesmen continually advertising what they are pleased to call Eastlake furniture, with the production of which I have had nothing whatever to do, and for the taste of which I should be very sorry to be considered responsible."

But the unauthorized use of Eastlake's name in America wasn't limited to furniture. In the 1880s and 1890s, enterprising developers realized that because mass transportation could provide easy, inexpensive commuting, workers no longer needed to live within walking distance of their jobs in the city. Commuter railroad lines were established into the near countryside, and the electric streetcar was developed. It was the birth of suburbia, and prosperous middle-class workers began to own their own homes.

These homes were built by the new balloon-frame construction method, in which light, precut pieces of lumber were held together by factory nails. This method was much less expensive, much quicker, and required far fewer workers than the earlier method, in which heavy pieces of lumber were connected by hand-cut pegs and mortise-and-tenon joints.

Featuring such modern amenities as indoor plumbing, central heating, and gas lighting, these new suburban homes were the last word in convenience as well as style. And what a style it was.

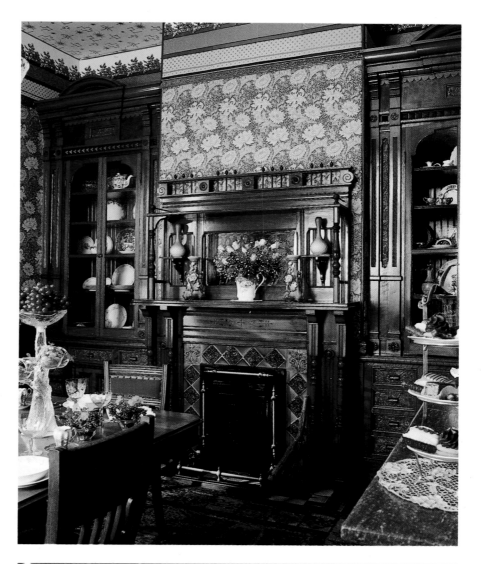

25
·
eastlake
style hardware

above right: Exuberance and abundance signify social standing in an Eastlake dining room, where the family's best crystal and finest porcelains are proudly displayed. The ornately carved china cabinet employs equally ornate latches and pulls.

right: In the profusion of ornamentation, it's almost hard to separate the drawer from the pull.

Most of us would call it Victorian. Architectural historians call it Queen Anne. The Queen Anne style originated in England in the 1870s, when architects looked back to the buildings of Queen Anne's reign (1702–1714) for inspiration. American architects and designers took the Queen Anne style, exaggerated it, embellished it, and called it Eastlake.

Queen Anne homes were themselves fantastic assemblages of architectural details: decorative turrets punctuated fish-scale shingle roofs while gables perched above sunburst clapboard walls ornamented with spindle work. A peek inside leaded-glass bay windows revealed high ceilings surrounded by friezes, stamped woodwork walls with ornamented picture moldings, and grand staircases ending in large newel posts decorated with carved globes or pineapples.

"Eastlake" style houses were even more elaborately decorated, with every exterior wall surface exhibiting applied wood carvings and cast-plaster reliefs. All this embellishment was made by machines, shipped to the location by rail, and glued into place by a carpenter.

27
.
eastlake
style hardware

opposite: Hardware doesn't have to be metal. Eastlake fruitwood dressers, like this walnut example, often have pulls made from the same wood.

right: The old lacquer on the brass cabinet latch gives it an aged patina. If cleaned, the original finish will remain.

above: More walnut furniture, this time in a bedroom set. Painted to look like ebony, the walnut drop pulls on the massive armoire have decorative brass back-plates. The keyhole covers are also walnut.

left: Known as a teardrop pull, this type of walnut drop pull with a decorative brass back-plate was very common on Eastlake furniture.

Predictably, Charles Eastlake had nothing kind to say about "his" style of home. When asked about the style in 1881 by an editor of *The California Architect and Building News,* Eastlake replied that he regretted that his name "should be associated . . . with a phase of taste in architecture and industrial art with which I can have no real sympathy, and which by all accounts seems to be extravagant and bizarre."

While Eastlake despised the furniture and houses that carried his name, he very well may have approved of the hardware used on the furniture and houses. Many of the patterns used to decorate American Eastlake door, window, and furniture hardware were based on patterns first developed by a colleague of Eastlake's, Christopher Dresser. Dresser shared Eastlake's concerns about the effect of the Industrial Revolution on standards of design and taste, but he believed that it was possible for mass-produced items to be tastefully decorated. He sold his decorative patterns—stylized forms derived from nature, with complex, repetitive geometric detailing— to manufacturers who used them for wallpaper, china, and silverwork. Dresser's 1873 *Principles of Decorative Design* became a standard reference work in industrial design schools.

The patterns decorating Eastlake style hardware are stylistically similar to the detailing on Eastlake furniture and architecture. Many patterns incorporate Japanese motifs, which became very popular once Japan opened to the West in 1853, after 216 years of isolation. The pulls on bedroom dressers often incorporated plant forms like trailing vines and bark. Doorplates and window hardware were made of iron, bronze, or brass; doorknobs were porcelain, glass, wood, or metal. Furniture hardware was usually brass, and sometimes nickel-plated.

Quite rare, this dresser has
an elaborate locking system.
The burled side panel is
actually hinged, fitting over the
drawers, and when it is locked
it also locks the drawers. The
keyhole covers and pulls are
brass, with typical geometric
Eastlake styling.

The softer side of Eastlake:
the marble-topped walnut
nightstand has a brass
single-hole drop pull.

Like the furniture and the homes on which it was used, American Eastlake style hardware was mass-produced in factories. The hardware was either cast, which entailed molten metals being poured into molds, or wrought, which meant a pattern was stamped into a thin piece of metal. Both methods had been used for centuries, but the cheaper and faster methods of production brought about by the Industrial Revolution enabled suburban homes across the country to be outfitted in this style.

The production of Eastlake architectural hardware signified a change in the use of American hardware. For the first time, all the hardware in a home was produced in the same pattern. Consumers could select from several different patterns, and their choice could outfit the entire house: the hardware on the exterior doors, the interior doors, the interior sliding doors, and the windows all matched.

opposite left: Even window hardware was decorated; in this instance an iron lock . . .

opposite right: . . . and a brass lift.

left: Porcelain doorknobs were often used with patterned doorplates or rosettes. This doorplate pattern was first manufactured in 1887 by the Lockwood Hardware Manufacturing Company. Employing Japanese-style design motifs, it is called the Broken Leaf.

33

eastlake
style hardware

The period in which the Eastlake style of hardware was produced saw the birth of the American hardware industry. Three of the most prominent companies in the history of American hardware, companies that would dominate the industry through the mid-twentieth century, were founded in Connecticut between 1858 and 1870. These companies, Russell and Erwin, P. & F. Corbin, and Yale and Towne, all featured decorative Eastlake hardware in their earliest trade catalogs.

Eastlake hardware was one of the first products of a newly industrialized America. As such, it reflected the exuberance and confidence of the time. In the coming decades, as the suburbs swelled and industrial methods improved, American hardware would continue to change, mirroring the times in which it was made.

victorian style hardware

This era represents the peak of the American decorative hardware industry. The Industrial Revolution and the resulting increased productivity leads to an explosion of choices, schools, patterns, finishes—and consequently the birth of planned obsolescence. Traditional styling—Gothic Revival, Italianate, and Queen Anne—symbolizes stability in a tumultuous period. Style runs rampant over function.

Innovations during the period include Henry Towne's *Locks and Builders' Hardware: A Handbook for Architects* (a thousand-page bible for consumers), inexpensive casting procedures, new finishing and plating techniques, and the perfection of an all-encompassing hardware aesthetic. Victorian doorknobs, doorplates, hinges, and furniture pulls are lavish, with complicated, swirling, floral patterns in relief.

35

The brass shines through the silver plating on this filigreed knob and plate. Filigree work was very common on Victorian door and furniture hardware. This pattern was manufactured around 1900 by the Hopkins and Dickenson Manufacturing Company of Darlington, New Jersey. Other companies produced very similar patterns— for instance, the Yale and Towne Antwerp pattern, part of the Louis XIII school.

When describing American decorative hardware, the label "Victorian" specifically signifies a period in time, not a style of hardware, although over time the label has come to signify a variety of styles that were all popular during the period. Today many different styles of decorative arts coexist under this general catchphrase. In Britain the period corresponded to the reign of Queen Victoria (1837–1901); in the United States it lasted slightly longer, until the First World War.

Between 1800 and 1900 the Industrial Revolution transformed America. The country began the century as a predominantly rural, agrarian society. By 1900 the nation's economy was overwhelmingly industrial.

As cities industrialized, social critics lamented the harshness of urban life. The country with its real soil, they claimed, was healthier for both body and soul. Developers took up the cry, and began subdividing farmland. Soon the growing middle class left the city centers, moving to apartment blocks (a new housing type in America) away from the factories or retreating even farther, into the expanding suburbs.

Suburban housing was a new challenge for American architects and builders in the final decades of the nineteenth century. Drawing from the example of their British counterparts, they built in a variety of traditional styles: Gothic Revival, Italianate, Stick-Style, Queen Anne. All these styles reflected the use of traditional motifs to symbolize stability during a tumultuous period.

Riots of colors and ornamentation, the exteriors of Victorian homes were irregularly shaped. Ample front porches embraced the landscape, and large picture windows brought nature inside.

The inside of a Victorian home burst with decorative objects. Some were handmade. But more and more they were mass-produced. And all were artistically arranged, demonstrating the family's individuality, its social standing, and its growing susceptibility to the mass marketing that accompanied burgeoning mass production.

No surface is left undecorated, as mass-produced bric-a-brac indicated good taste in the proper Victorian parlor. A portrait of Queen Victoria watches over the swirl of patterns, textures, and shapes.

These decorative objects also proved that members of the family had good taste, which to Victorians meant that the family was morally upright. The more bric-a-brac, the better the taste, and the more virtue. It was no coincidence that department stores (a new retail innovation) hired interior designers to set up model rooms and to give women advice on how to fill their homes with the very mass-produced examples of propriety and affluence that were bursting off the shelves.

The concept of good taste extended to decorative hardware. As elaborate buildings were constructed to reflect the solidity of the past, the hardware in those buildings was equally elaborate and equally influenced by the past.

While the genesis of most of the hardware styles produced during the Victorian period, including the Eastlake style, was English, the culmination of these styles was born in the design departments of the developing American hardware industry. American industry was becoming America's tastemaker.

In 1870 the Metallic Compression Casting Company of Boston invented a new method of casting that made ornamental hardware both economically feasible and artistically pleasing. Two years later the Russell and Erwin Manufacturing Company of New Britain, Connecticut, bought the Metallic Compression Casting Company and hired a professional designer. Competing companies also hired designers, and soon there were thousands of patterns of hardware to decorate the proper Victorian building. The flowering of American hardware had begun.

Hardware manufacturers weren't shy about promoting their pieces of functional beauty. In 1904, Henry Towne, the owner of the Yale and Towne Manufacturing Company, compiled *Locks and Builders'*

above: In this parlor, the filigreed pocket doorplate holds its own amid all the flourishes.

right: Fancy metal finishes were the pride of the Victorian hardware industry. This pocket door pull was originally silver-plated brass; over years the plating has worn off and the brass shines through. Compare this pull with the Eastlake pocket door pull (p. 20) and the differences between the two styles will become apparent.

using victorian hardware

finding it

Victorian hardware can be found all over, but the greatest concentration is in the Midwest.

While high-quality, cast-brass Victorian hardware is becoming scarce, pressed-iron and -brass Victorian hardware is still relatively easy to find.

A few patterns of Victorian door hardware are being reproduced.

There is quite a bit of Victorian cabinet and furniture hardware, particularly bin pulls and glass cabinet knobs, being reproduced.

practical considerations

You may find all the hardware you need in a single pattern, but because there were so many different manufacturers' finishes for Victorian hardware, the finishes on the individual pieces may vary widely. If you want all the pieces to have the same finish, take them to a plating company and have them plated in the finish of your choice.

The silver-plated ball-tipped hinge is similar in feeling to the filigreed knob and plate (p. 34) and the pocket doorplate (p. 39). Compare it to the Eastlake steeple-tipped hinge (p. 19) for a graphic representation of the differences between the two styles.

Be careful when matching Victorian bin pulls. They may look alike at first glance, but they were manufactured in many different sizes and with some very subtle styling differences.

When using glass cabinet knobs with a center screw, be sure not to tighten the nut on the inside of the cabinet too tight—too much pressure will cause the glass knob to crack.

decorative considerations

With its floral styling, Victorian door hardware softens almost any room. In addition to being used in Victorian interiors, it is particularly appropriate in romantic studies, bedrooms, and bathrooms. Victorian door hardware does not easily work in more structured, tailored environments like Arts and Crafts or mid-century homes.

Traditional Victorian glass cabinet knobs and bin pulls have enjoyed a renewed recognition in the past decade and are now used in almost any style kitchen, from the most traditional to the most modern.

Glass doorknobs, which were used most widely in the 1920s and '30s, work well with Victorian doorplates. Original glass knobs are relatively easy to find, and some companies are manufacturing quality reproductions in a variety of colors. You can also buy new glass doorknobs at any home center, but they are of much lower quality than the originals or good reproductions.

Hardware: A Handbook for Architects. A good Victorian, Towne sincerely believed that truth and beauty could shine through inanimate objects. An unabashed industrialist, he believed his objects were the most truthful and beautiful. His thousand-page book was designed to prove his point to his customers. And if it helped to sell a few thousand more locks . . . so be it.

Not surprisingly, Towne used the Yale and Towne line of decorative hardware to illustrate his conception of beautiful and appropriate hardware. In the nineteenth century the academic study of art history became systematized, and scholars began classifying all ornament as belonging to particular "schools." The hardware industry followed this system, and divided its decorative pieces into different historical schools.

top left: Delicate filigree knobs illustrate the Victorian interest in complex patterns.

bottom left: The brass keyhole is a mass of raised swirls.

above: Victorian dining rooms were dominated by massive oak sideboards. The finest quality Victorian furniture featured cast-brass knobs, drawer pulls, and keyhole covers. On this example, the knobs on the right are original to the piece, while the knobs on the left—which are stylistically similar—were added sometime later. Subtlety matters when playing hardware detective: note that the knobs on the right match the patina of the keyhole covers and drawer pulls, a sure clue that they were the original knobs.

An extensive butler's pantry illustrates the changing role of women. For the first time, middle-class women did their own cooking, which meant that kitchens needed to be a little bit nicer and more comfortable than they had been in the past, when they had been the exclusive domain of servants. Also, the many-course meals that were standard during the Victorian period required a lot of dishes, and a lot of storage space. Here, nickel-plated brass latches and bin pulls march along the storage cabinets.

In 1904 Yale and Towne divided its hardware into twenty-four schools, each of which was composed of dozens of different patterns. The schools ran the gamut from Greek to Flemish Renaissance to Indian to German Gothic to Japanese to Modern. The Colonial school alone featured fifty patterns (all named for geographic locations important in colonial America), almost half of which provided both builders' and cabinet hardware.

In the chapter entitled "Art Metal Work and Ornament," architect W. W. Kent outlined the role of hardware in the home. He explained that beautiful decorative hardware appealed "above all, to the lady of the house, as affording an opportunity where an educated taste and the judicious expenditure of money yield a more effective result and a more lasting pleasure than can be procured at equal cost in any other way."

Also in Towne's book, noted architectural historian Montgomery Schuyler described at length the unsuitability of all hardware produced before the 1870s. He wrote that it was the work of "pattern-makers who were entirely untutored, either in the principles or in the historical examples of ornamental design." While "Eastlake hardware was an improvement upon what had preceded it . . . its forms failed to commend themselves as beautiful or appropriate, and now appear hopelessly antiquated."

Modern, beautiful hardware, Schuyler believed, must be scholastic, it must look to the past in order to harmonize with the building in which it appears. Only by studying "the schools of all times and lands: delicate Byzantine tracery, bold and rugged Romanesque work, the later Gothic, our own Colonial and many others" could designers create appropriate contemporary hardware.

right: Scrolls, shells, and cartouches—all in a single drawer pull. Consisting of a filigreed back-plate, two eyes, and an arched bail pull, Victorian drawer pulls almost always measured three inches between the holes.

opposite: Unusual in that it combines two pieces of furniture commonly found in Victorian bedrooms into one, this oak piece is both a dresser and a washstand. The filigreed pressed-brass drawer pulls and cabinet knobs are in the most common pattern used on mass-marketed furniture.

Regardless of the school of ornament to which they are attributed, Victorian hardware patterns are very similar to one another. The overall effect is lavish, with complicated, swirling floral designs in relief. Reflecting the fanciful house exteriors and cluttered interiors, not a surface of the hardware is left undecorated.

One of the great accomplishments of the American hardware industry during this period was the development of different finishing processes. In the mid-1800s metalworkers began experimenting with plating processes, where a "plate" of a malleable metal like silver, nickel, or copper is applied to the surface of a sturdier metal like iron, brass, or bronze. This changes the base metal's appearance.

In the 1880s and 1890s chemists working for hardware manufacturers developed finishes that actually altered the chemical composition of the base metal. Special finishes were desirable because they could further ensure the harmony of the hardware with the building in which it was used; both the styling of the

hardware and its finish could invoke images of the past. Yale and Towne offered dozens of different finishes, many with grandiose names like Pompeiian Bronze, Butler's Silver, or Statuary Bronze Verde Antique.

Another development in American hardware during the Victorian period was directly tied to the changing role of middle-class women. In previous decades, wealthy women didn't spend any time in the kitchen, because they had servants. Working-class women, who did their own cooking, were concerned with subsistence, not with interior decoration. But in the 1880s and 1890s, middle-class suburban housewives did most of their own housework and cooking, spending hours preparing elaborate multicourse meals.

All this cooking required a lot of time, space, and storage. Hence the birth of decorative, coordinated kitchen hardware for "the lady of the house." The cup-shaped pulls on storage bins were either plain or nickel-plated brass or iron. Storage cabinets usually featured nickel-plated brass cabinet latches or glass knobs and handles, which were mass-produced in brilliant pinks, greens, and blues. An up-to-date kitchen at the turn of the last century was a coordinated kitchen because its hardware, not its appliances, carried the decorating scheme.

Bathrooms in Victorian homes symbolized affluence and were a source of great pride because indoor plumbing was far from universal at the time. Plumbing fixtures were made of nickel-plated brass. Bathroom accessories like towel bars, soap dishes, and toothbrush holders were either nickel-plated brass or vitreous china. Built-in cabinets and medicine chests used the same glass knobs and handles found in kitchens.

American hardware mass-produced in the late nineteenth and early twentieth centuries is a three-dimensional embodiment of the contradictions of the Victorian period. Swept up in a tidal wave of technological advances and high-pressure mass marketing, Americans embraced the new world wrapped in stylish designs from the past. Future designers would concern themselves with the relationship between form and function and the expression of technology through design, but for the Victorians familiar motifs from the past symbolized the moral rectitude of the present and provided comfort in the face of an uncertain future.

arts and crafts style hardware

Initially a philosophy decrying the excesses of the Industrial Revolution, the Arts and Crafts movement in England ended up giving birth to a mass-produced American design style—and a "handmade" one at that.

Featuring function over form, the Arts and Crafts style of hardware harkens back to the past. It is simple, stylized, and, in the case of furniture hardware, never used solely for decoration. Hardware was viewed as a "useful art."

Innovations include new mechanical and chemical "antiquing" processes; the proliferation of the use of copper; *The Craftsman*, Gustav Stickley's journal of the movement; the bungalow for the masses; and the designs of Frank Lloyd Wright and Charles and Henry Greene for the custom market.

Always looking toward the past, the style is functional, simple, and handmade.

49

Arts and Crafts door hardware was usually quite plain.

The Industrial Revolution swept through the world like an enormous wave. Before the wave hit a culture, few could imagine its consequences. Once the wave did hit, everyone was swept up in its power. After it passed, nothing would ever be the same.

left: Open pocket doors between the living room and the sitting room create one large "great" room, a staple in Arts and Crafts homes.

above: Plain bin pulls open the drawers on the cabinet. The cutouts were for labels, which could be used to identify the drawer's contents.

below: The plain brass switchplate carries the simplicity of the Arts and Crafts style. Two-button light switches were used through the 1930s, regardless of the style of the home.

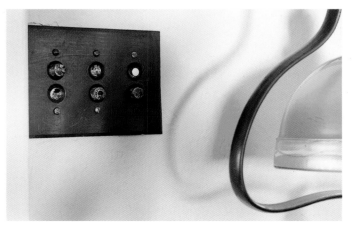

As the Industrial Revolution hit its stride in Britain, America was several decades behind in industrial development. So as British social critics like Charles Eastlake were condemning the decorative excesses made possible by the Industrial Revolution, Americans were just beginning to embrace those excesses. The initial embrace led to Eastlake style hardware, which was the first American mass-produced hardware, as well as a three-dimensional representation of excess.

Thirty years and countless Victorian era excesses later, Americans too began to yearn for a simpler, more honest time. And American stylemakers did just what they had done in the past. They looked to England, co-opted an English style, gave it a different spin, and created a uniquely American style of hardware.

The English reformers who started the Arts and Crafts movement were concerned about the effect of the factory system upon the individual worker. By reducing the creation of clothing, vases, or chairs to a series of rote tasks, mass production lessened an individual's role in the final outcome of the product. Each worker was responsible for a single step in the process, instead of being involved in the entire process from start to finish. Separating the worker from the final product, the reformers argued, degraded the final product and the act of labor. The way to reverse this deterioration was through small-scale, worker-owned industrialism.

The best known of these early reformers, William Morris, established the firm Morris, Marshall, Faulkner and Co. (later Morris and Company) in London in 1861. With the goal of uniting all the arts, the collaborative venture produced furniture, stained glass, embroidery, painted tile, table glass, and metalwork.

Following Morris's example, the Art Workers Guild was founded in London in 1884. The guild brought together architects, painters,

above: Stickley furniture abounds in an exquisite Arts and Crafts living room. The reclining Morris chair in the foreground, the bookcase, the drop-front secretary next to the fireplace, and the side tables were all made by Gustav Stickley. The copper table lamp is by Dirk Van Erp, a prominent Arts and Crafts coppersmith, whose Van Erp Studio in San Francisco was active until 1949.

right: A Tiffany lily lamp on a Gustav Stickley bookcase. The candlesticks are by Robert Jarvie, a Chicago metalsmith whose career exemplifies the Arts and Crafts emphasis on the transformative power of handicraft. A clerk in the Chicago city government, Jarvie taught himself metalsmithing. By 1905, after twelve years as an amateur metalsmith, he abandoned his bureaucratic career and opened the Jarvie Shop, where he employed a team of craftsmen. He became a major influence in the Chicago Arts and Crafts Society.

and designers for lectures, debates, and the demonstration of craft processes. These artisans felt that work not only was an act of economic sustenance, but should be an act of creative sustenance and an expression of joyfulness. Beautiful, practical objects—the "useful arts"—were the expression of honest labor. In 1887 the guild became the Arts and Crafts Society, thereby naming the movement.

English Arts and Crafts proponents lectured widely in the United States, quickly gaining American followers. The Boston Society of Arts and Crafts was founded in June 1897, and soon there were similar societies in Chicago, New York, Minneapolis, and Detroit. These groups spread Arts and Crafts ideals through salesrooms, exhibitions, classes, and periodicals devoted to the useful arts of metalwork, textiles, bookbinding, pottery, and woodworking.

Initially, the Arts and Crafts movement in the United States was a philosophy, not a style. Arts and Crafts advocates sought to free workers from the deadening monotony of the factories. Communal

opposite: The cabinet and floor lamp are both by Gustav Stickley. Stickley's attention to details, shown in the dovetailing on the cabinet and the hammered copper pull, gave his furniture the appearance of being handmade. The lamp shade is made of Steuben glass; while contemporary to the lamp, it is not original to it.

right: While they may have been produced by machines, the patinated finish makes the hinges and pull on the Stickley bookcase look handwrought.

workshops, they believed, would enable a worker to practice his or her craft and to own the means of production. The craftsperson would be creatively and economically sustained, and the useful arts produced would be the result of moral, honest labor.

As the American Arts and Crafts movement gained momentum, decorative objects as disparate as teapots and tablecloths exhibited similar styling. Arts and Crafts pieces incorporated flowing, natural forms in simple arrangements, with the styling becoming simpler and more stylized as time went on.

Arts and Crafts objects always expressed their function in their design. In direct opposition to the Victorian habit of disguising an object in a mass of flourishes and flounces, an Arts and Crafts teaspoon was obviously a teaspoon, and a dress obviously a dress.

Furniture maker Gustav Stickley was one of the best-known American Arts and Crafts advocates. He began his career in the 1880s in upstate New York, where he manufactured his own mixture of Shaker, Queen Anne, and Colonial furniture. His first exposure to Arts and Crafts furniture was during an 1898 trip to England.

Back in the United States, Stickley transformed himself from an entrepreneur into a craftsman. He founded the Craftsman Workshops, which he modeled on Morris and Company. Profit-sharing craftspeople made furniture, worked in metal and leather, and helped publish *The Craftsman,* a journal devoted to spreading the Arts and Crafts message.

At the 1900 Grand Rapids Furniture Fair he exhibited his New Furniture to a large audience for the first time. The furniture's simple, straight lines appealed to the public's nostalgia for the simplicity of earlier eras, and soon similar lines of furniture were

Wood tones dominate this Arts and Crafts sitting room. The door hardware is plain yet substantial.

being produced by dozens of manufacturers in Grand Rapids, Chicago, Indianapolis, Cincinnati, and New York State.

Stickley sold his oak furniture, with the distinctive rayed-grain pattern produced by quartering whole logs, through a mail-order catalog and in stores across the country. He often implied that the furniture was totally handmade. His claim is impossible to believe, based on the sheer quantity of pieces produced, with thousands of pieces existing a century after they were made.

Elbert Hubbard, the founder of Roycroft, another Arts and Crafts workshop in upstate New York, claimed that each of his pieces of furniture was completely handmade by a single woodworker. Upon

above left: The inlay detail in the dining table exhibits the sensuous styling of Art Nouveau, a late-nineteenth-century European style that lent many stylistic influences to the Arts and Crafts movement. The soft detailing of the table provides a pleasing counterpoint to the sturdiness of the Arts and Crafts sideboard.

opposite: Echoing the solidity of the sideboard, this is a very common Arts and Crafts handle.

using arts and crafts hardware

finding it

It is very difficult to find handmade, highly detailed original Arts and Crafts door hardware. The original hardware that does exist can be found in the Midwest and on the West Coast.

It is also difficult to find original Arts and Crafts furniture hardware. In the past twenty years there has been renewed interest in and appreciation for Arts and Crafts furniture, so the original hardware is rarely separated from its original piece.

Some companies are reproducing Arts and Crafts door and furniture hardware, but, like the original, it can be very expensive because of the meticulous craftsmanship involved.

practical considerations

If you're having trouble finding original Arts and Crafts door hardware, any undecorated, rectilinear hardware will carry out the Arts and Crafts feeling.

Square or pyramidal wood knobs (quarter-sawn wood ones are the best) are a good alternative to original Arts and Crafts furniture hardware. Very plain dark brass or iron eyes and bails would also work.

decorative considerations

Simple Arts and Crafts hardware blends in with almost any interior design scheme. It can lend a very tailored look, or it can be an unobtrusive accent in more elaborately embellished rooms.

above: All the elements of the Arts and Crafts style in one bungalow entrance: art glass, art pottery, a copper-and-mica lamp, copper accessories, and a desk by L. and J. G. Stickley. Gustav Stickley's brothers, Leopold and John George, worked with Gustav early in their careers, then branched off and formed the L. and J. G. Stickley company.

right: Detailing is the cornerstone of Arts and Crafts styling. This handle by L. and J. G. Stickley becomes the focal point for the plain quarter-sawn oak desk.

above: The entire kitchen was designed to match the two cabinets on the right, which were designed by noted Arts and Crafts architects Charles and Henry Greene. The cabinets feature an unusual use of hardware: the latches are actually casement window fasteners. The doorknob and doorplate are very common in Arts and Crafts interiors. To the left of the stove shelf, a tiny milk-glass cabinet knob sits on the pantry door.

left: The Victorian octagonal milk-glass cabinet knob on the pantry door in the Arts and Crafts kitchen represents a hardware truism: rarely did a home incorporate one single style of hardware. Styles exist on a continuum, and it was not at all unusual for a builder or architect to incorporate both past and current styles.

visiting Roycroft, a contemporary journalist suggested otherwise: he counted at least half a dozen power tools in the workshop.

These companies—and the scores of others producing furniture lines they called "Quaint," "New Art," "Modern," "Mission," "Craftsman," "Russmore," "Arts and Crafts," and "Hand Craft"—used hardware to give their furniture the illusion of handcraftsmanship. Hand-hammered (or machine-made to look hand-hammered) strap hinges, pulls, and escutcheons invoked the feeling of an earlier time.

In a 1910 catalog Stickley explained why he first made hardware: "The first need was for a metal trim which would harmonize in character with the furniture, as none of the glittering, fragile metal then in vogue was possible in connection with its straight severe lines and plain surfaces. So I opened a metalwork department. . . ."

Made of brass, iron, copper, and sometimes wood, Arts and Crafts furniture hardware was always functional. Unlike Victorian furniture hardware, it was never used exclusively for decoration.

left: Another example of decorative styles in transition: on an exterior thumb-lever handle, the hand hammering and square bolt covers are definitive Arts and Crafts details, while the scrolls on the handle ends are strong Victorian motifs.

opposite: Hardware featuring figures of animals was mass-produced as early as 1865. This wonderful thumb-lever handle featuring a beaver hard at work shows its Arts and Crafts roots in its "handmade" quality and the attention to organic detailing.

Metalworkers hammered hardware to create the illusion of age. They also experimented with different finishing techniques to give the pieces an "antique" finish. With the help of chemicals, iron could be made to look like copper, a much more expensive metal.

Arts and Crafts furniture hardware was available separately from the furniture, and through a variety of sources. Periodicals like *The Craftsman* printed patterns for home craftspeople to make their own hardware. Crafts workshops like the Frost Arts and Crafts Workshop of Dayton, Ohio, sold kits for furniture hardware. The Craftsman Workshops and Roycroft sold furniture hardware through the mail. By the 1920s large hardware manufacturers offered Arts and Crafts furniture hardware as part of their regular inventory.

The heart of the Arts and Crafts lifestyle—and ultimately of the useful arts—was the home. Late-nineteenth-century English Arts and Crafts architects turned away from the industrial present and sought to develop an architectural style based on English tradition. They turned toward nature in their use of natural materials and back to the Middle Ages in their use of Gothic motifs like pointed arches and iron hardware.

The first American Arts and Crafts architects followed their English counterparts' lead. Leaded-glass windows, pointed arches, and half-timbering imported a nostalgic view of English building history to American soil.

Soon American innovators began to rely less on traditional English surface motifs as they sought to develop an Arts and Crafts style all their own. The celebration of the natural landscape became the center of the American Arts and Crafts architectural style. Prominent architects such as Frank Lloyd Wright and the firm of Henry Mather Greene and Charles Sumner Greene designed low-lying, horizontal homes that seemed to flow out of the landscape, with their function expressed by their design.

Wright and the Greene brothers designed for a clientele that could afford custom homes. The real architectural innovation of the Arts and Crafts movement was the development of a new building type for the booming middle class: the bungalow. The bungalow originated in British-occupied India, where it was a one-story thatched hut with a central-hall plan. The name bungalow comes from the Indian word *"bangla,"* which denoted both a common dwelling type and the geographic region of Bengal.

The earliest bungalows in the United States were country retreats. By the time the American Arts and Crafts movement hit its stride, bungalows were unpretentious one or one-and-a-half story houses with sweeping, overhanging eaves and large porches. The building booms of the 1910s and 1920s were clothed in suburban tracts of inexpensive, middle-class single-family bungalows.

In a jumble of Arts and Crafts drawer handles, the handsome detailing shines through.

Gustav Stickley was one of the most vocal advocates of the bungalow. In *The Craftsman,* he published drawings for what he called Craftsman Homes (the term "craftsman" is now used as a generic description of an Arts and Crafts bungalow). The plans for these homes could also be purchased from the Craftsman Workshops.

Stickley wasn't alone in realizing that the bungalow fit very well with the demand for middle-class housing. Between 1905 and 1925, marketing bungalows almost became an industry in itself.

Popular magazines like the *Ladies' Home Journal* printed articles about the joys of bungalow living. The Sherwin-Williams paint company published brochures detailing the proper color and furniture choices for bungalow interiors, and each month the Seattle-based *Bungalow Magazine* offered complete working drawings for a bungalow. In keeping with the handicraft spirit of the Arts and Crafts movement, Sears, Roebuck and Company and the Aladdin Company sold do-it-yourself kits for as little as $400.

Although not all bungalows were Arts and Crafts in style (Stickley himself developed designs for saltbox farmhouses and "Modern Colonial" homes and Sears had a kit for any architectural mood), the majority of bungalows took on some Arts and Crafts styling. Most plans featured a "great" room, combining living room, dining room, and den. Built-in furniture was used as a space-saving device and to further the sense of the interior as one flowing room.

Just as bungalows were designed to blend in with their natural surroundings, the Arts and Crafts door and window hardware produced from the turn of the century until 1920 was designed to blend in with the unpretentious interiors. Made of cast or wrought iron or brass, the hardware was rectilinear and blocky, usually without surface decoration.

An L. and J. G. Stickley hammered copper keyhole plate and ring pull.

Doorplates were rectangular, with either straight or beveled edges. Doorknobs were usually round with flat or slightly domed faces, but sometimes the faces of the knobs were composed of planes forming a pyramid.

As in Arts and Crafts furniture hardware, hammered copper was occasionally used, most often for lighting fixtures and in custom door hardware. Also as in the furniture hardware, manufacturers experimented with different finishes to give the illusion of age. Exterior doors on larger bungalows often featured hammered strap hinges, once again a reference to the past.

By the second decade of the twentieth century, the American Arts and Crafts movement had lost most of its theoretical edge. Snug in their bungalows with mass-produced hardware, middle-class home owners didn't care about the origins of the Arts and Crafts movement or William Morris and his concept of "joyful work." Nevertheless, some of Morris's spirit lived on in the mass-produced hardware: its simple lines expressed its function without any extraneous embellishment. In this way, decorative hardware was the epitome of the Arts and Crafts' useful arts.

revival style hardware

Borrowing themes and forms from the past, the Revival styles of design sought to elicit the romance and security of long-ago times and faraway places right in the heart of booming American suburbia. Using techniques developed to create the "handmade" look of Arts and Crafts style hardware, manufacturers mass-produced simple, "handmade," "historical" iron and brass pieces by the millions.

History, not philosophy, dictated the forms of this style. And form, not function, drove the overall aesthetic. Not surprisingly, the birth of historic preservation and restoration programs was the dominant innovation of the movement. Hardware for the Revival styles was rustic, quaint, old world, and romantic.

During the fifty years in which buildings were built in the various Revival styles, America fought the Spanish-American War, the First World War, suffered through the Depression, and entered into the Second World War. It's little wonder that while the Arts and Crafts style sprang from a philosophical movement, the Revival styles were born in the collective psyche of Americans yearning for a simpler, safer past.

69

Revival style hardware, like this Spanish Colonial Revival example, emphasized romance. This set, a very common pattern for door hardware, shows the signs of time. The blackened patina can be cleaned with fine steel wool and metal cleaner, revealing the original nickel-plated finish.

In this 1928 Spanish Colonial Revival, all the hardware was custom-made. In the living room, extraordinary iron casement fasteners accent the floor-to-ceiling windows. **detail, above:** Old world romance finds its way onto 1920s casement fasteners.

During this period America's population increased by more than 60 percent and the exodus from the cities to the suburbs began in earnest. And while some were looking to the future with optimism in the styles of Art Deco and Streamline Moderne, the majority of the middle class was dreaming of a simpler past in their own suburban Colonial Revival bungalow.

Much of the current American landscape was determined by the results of the 1920 census, which revealed that only half of all Americans owned their own homes. Concerned by this statistic, the federal government established programs to provide affordable housing for the American middle class. These programs created a

A Tudor Revival bungalow exemplifies the picturesque quality of the Revival styles. While it was undoubtedly mass-produced, the thumb-lever handle on the front door looks handwrought, and the square bolt covers match the joinery details on the door. The blackened iron handle on the door into the dining room furthers the rustic tone.

Atmosphere abounds in a Spanish Colonial Revival dining room.

nationwide real estate boom, with the land surrounding city centers quickly developed for suburban housing in the early 1920s.

Speculative developers wielded enormous aesthetic power as they laid out the new suburbs. Not only did they make far-reaching decisions about street width, sewer size, open land, and the provision of transportation, they also determined the styles of homes people would own. And sensing the collective uneasiness just under the surface of the Roaring Twenties, these developers chose period revivals of familiar, romantic forms. Block after block of Colonial Revival, English Tudor, French Norman, and Spanish Colonial Revival homes sprouted in empty fields.

Tudor and Colonial Revival homes were common throughout the country. In certain areas, local architectural traditions determined which revival style would be used: Mediterranean (a mélange of Italian, Moorish, and Spanish elements) in Florida, German in Pennsylvania, Spanish Colonial in California. Not surprisingly this renewed interest in historical styles gave birth to the first historic preservation and restoration programs in the 1920s.

Through the decades, the Colonial Revival style has been the most enduring style of American suburban home. The square, symmetrical form topped by a peaked roof and featuring a doorway flanked by columns came to America on the *Mayflower.* Over the next centuries the style's simple lines and details conveyed stability and familiarity.

opposite: *¡Viva la romance!* in a Spanish Colonial Revival kitchen. Porcelain towel bar ends were widely used in kitchens and bathrooms during the period.

above left: While the details— hammering, twisting, careful incising—look handwrought, the nickel-plated brass handle is actually machine-made.

left: This interior thumb-lever handle has the same detailing as the drawer handles above.

using revival hardware

finding it

Elaborate, ornate original Revival style homes are usually restored, not demolished, which means that the best Revival style hardware is often difficult to find.

There are some companies making good reproduction Revival style hardware. The higher quality the hardware, the more expensive it is.

practical considerations

If you can't find ornate Spanish Colonial or Mediterranean Revival style door hardware, consider using iron or nickel-plated brass levers in place of doorknobs for an old world look.

Glass doorknobs were also used widely during this period, so they may be an option. For a Spanish Colonial or Mediterranean Revival look, use them with plain iron or nickel-plated brass doorplates or rosettes. A Tudor Revival home could use glass knobs with plain iron doorplates or rosettes. Glass doorknobs with iron doorplates or rosettes would work for a rustic Colonial Revival home; use glass knobs and simple brass doorplates or rosettes for a more refined Colonial Revival.

Thumb—or gate—latches are a good look for rustic Revival style homes, particularly Colonial Revival homes.

decorative considerations

Just as the manufacturers of original Revival style hardware blurred the distinctions among the different Revival styles—Spanish Colonial, etc.—so can you. The word to remember when using Revival style hardware is "romance"; while Revival style hardware works well in lush old world interiors, it would definitely be less successful in more tailored homes.

Monterey furniture hardware was designed especially for the pieces it embellished. The hardware was often painted to match the finish of the wood, as on this sideboard.

Monterey furniture in a sunny living room. The wall sconce and curtain hardware are typically Spanish Colonial Revival, while the plain brass door hardware is not.

In the 1920s and 1930s Colonial Revival and smaller, more casual Cape Cod homes dotted the new suburbs. Drawing upon tradition, these homes had very plain brass hardware, reproductions of the hardware that the early colonists imported from England. Some of the more "rustic" Colonial Revival homes featured simple black iron hardware, which recalled "the atmosphere of the forge, the romance of iron and laborious methods of hand work," according to a 1931 catalog from the P. & F. Corbin hardware company.

opposite: Plentiful patterns in a Spanish Colonial Revival bathroom: the design on the tiles is echoed in the painted doors, and the design on the doorknob is echoed in the cabinet knobs.

above: The knobs on the built-in cabinets have the same incised detailings as the doorknob.

right: Patinated with age, the brass hardware consists of a knob, a rosette behind the knob, and a thumb turn. Thumb turns, also called privacy locks, were commonly used in bathrooms and bedrooms.

Other styles of revival architecture also invoked a simpler, more charming past. Decorative accents like half-timbering, elaborate window grilles, hand-painted tile, and rustic lanterns gave each home in a single neighborhood a sense of individuality and romance. Inside, these "quaint" houses all shared the same basic floor plan and were outfitted with the most up-to-date electrical appliances.

Period Revival hardware was mass-produced to look handwrought. Special finishes were also used to give it a rustic patina. Unlike Arts and Crafts hardware, period Revival hardware was rustic not for philosophical reasons, but for aesthetic reasons.

In most cases, the hardware was interchangeable across styles. The P. & F. Corbin catalog explained that the door lever and strap hinges used on a Spanish Colonial home would be equally appropriate on an English Tudor home:

opposite: A wrought-iron grapevine covers the casement windows in a bedroom.

above left: A detail of the grape.

above right: The intricacy of the hand-forged casement fastener matches that of the grille that covers it.

left: Although made in the 1920s, the magnificent wrought-iron ring pull is based on European designs used throughout the Middle Ages. History and romance intermingle while opening a door.

opposite left: A finely detailed cabinet knob . . .

opposite right: . . . matches an adjacent doorknob.

In some instances, though, it is extremely difficult to draw definite lines of classification because of the curious commingling of design motives in many of the old schools. However, each piece carries an unmistakable relation to traditional architecture and one may choose from several patterns for any particular style with the assurance that each will reflect the spirit of its surroundings.

The romance didn't end at the front door. Hand-crafted mass-produced hardware was used throughout the home, as were hand-painted tiles and rustic light fixtures.

Many people furnished their homes with furniture influenced by the architecture. This practice was particularly prevalent in Southern California, where waitresses lived in Spanish Colonial Revival bungalow apartments and movie stars lived in Spanish Colonial Revival mansions.

Monterey brand furniture, produced by the Mason Manufacturing Company of Los Angeles from 1929 to 1943, blended motifs from the Arts and Crafts era with romantic styling from Spain. Rough cast-iron drawer pulls and large strap hinges reinforced the old world feeling. Monterey furniture became so popular that Sears, Roebuck and Company began producing its own version, the La Fiesta line.

The romance of the Revival styles—and the romance of home ownership—came to an abrupt halt with the Depression. Homes for the affluent continued to be built, but the rapid suburban expansion of the 1920s was over. After the Depression suburban development continued, but architectural styles and the decorative arts took a drastic shift away from the nostalgic.

art deco and streamline moderne style hardware

85

Art Deco was the first comprehensive American decorative style that originated in France, not in Britain. It was also the first decorative style that looked toward the future rather than the past. After several years of visual luxury and extravagance, Art Deco merged with the Bauhaus-born International style to create Streamline Moderne.

Both styles were used predominantly in custom homes and commercial interiors rather than in middle-class homes. Mr. and Mrs. Average American sat in an Art Deco movie theater and watched Jean Harlow on the screen as she vamped in her Streamline Moderne boudoir; then, when the curtain fell they returned to their English Tudor Revival home.

Innovations of the period included the use of new materials such as Bakelite, Lucite, aluminum, and stainless steel; the introduction of cylindrical lock-sets; and "hardware-less" design.

Elegant and sensuous, Art Deco and Streamline Moderne hardware was designed with an eye to the future.

The nickel-plated brass ziggurat knob and plate typifiy the geometric styling of the Art Deco and Streamline Moderne styles.

Art Deco, called le Style Moderne in France and Art Moderne in England, embodied movement—away from the past, away from war, toward a future based on optimism and energy. The style was born in turn-of-the-century Paris, which was alive with artists, interior designers, and industrial designers who used government-financed exhibitions to show their work to one another and the public. Feeling that previous exhibitions had overlooked the decorative arts in favor of painting, a group of designers formed the Société des Artistes

The luxury and extravagance of Art Deco: a built-in burled walnut bedroom suite with marble-topped nightstands.

87
.
art deco and
s t r e a m l i n e
m o d e r n e
style hardware

The sensuous shape of the
nightstand is repeated in the
cream-colored Bakelite pull.
A resin material that was the
precursor to modern plastics,
Bakelite was used extensively
during the 1920s and 1930s.

Décorateurs. The goal of the society was to set up an international
exhibition of contemporary decorative arts as quickly as possible.

Years went by as the group lobbied the government for funding. By
the time financing was secured and the exhibition set for 1915, the
First World War had broken out. After the armistice, the plans were
resurrected as a way to restore France's glory and trading position,
but shortages delayed the opening until 1925.

above: The nickel-plated faucets, shelf, towel bar, and grab bar only intensify the luxuriousness of the sunken tub. Note the female figures amid the palm fronds on the wall.

above right: The Jazz Age lives on in etched windows by Lalique, the renowned French glass company.

right: It's hard to tell where the glass of the shower door ends and the sleek shower-door handle begins. The ultimate in coordination: the custom shower-door handle matches the door handles in the bathroom.

opposite: All the fixtures—the sink, the medicine chest, the marble shelves, the grille, the faucets— were designed specifically for the bathroom.

The official exhibition rules for the 1925 Exposition des Arts Décoratifs et Industriels Modernes stated that the show was "open to all manufacturers whose product is artistic in character and shows clearly modern tendencies." Drawing upon influences from the revolutionary modern arts movements of the early twentieth century such as Cubism and Futurism, designers from dozens of countries brought their modern tendencies to Paris, setting the future course of the decorative arts.

More than one hundred pavilions showcased innovations in metal, glass, ceramics, musical instruments, scientific equipment, textiles, embroidery, jewelry, hairdressing, flowers, clothing, leatherwork, printing, and architecture. The emphasis was on ornament and elegance, and most of the furniture and architecture was very highly decorated and made of the finest materials.

In the past it had sometimes taken decades for European styles to migrate to America. But because of improved communications and the inherent forward-looking allure of the style, Art Deco reached America almost immediately. A group of items from the 1925 Paris exhibition was already touring American museums in 1926, starting at the Metropolitan Museum of Art in New York. In 1928 Macy's department store organized the "First International Exposition of Art in Industry," showcasing European work. One hundred thousand people visited this show in the first week. The next year the Metropolitan organized its own exhibition, "The Architect and the International Arts," in which eight modernist architects each designed a complete room setting, using furniture and other components designed by them and produced by leading manufacturers.

Embracing Art Deco, American designers decorated pottery, silverware, lacquerware, furniture, book jackets, and clothing with

left: A dressing room displays the style of the times: Art Deco details take on some Spanish Colonial Revival overtones. The grille is definitely Deco . . .

above: . . . but the nickel-plated brass knobs and hinges blend the two styles.

the new style of the Jazz Age. They incorporated non-European traditions to make the style particularly their own, finding inspiration from the geometric stylization of Native American arts, the pre-Columbian arts, and the architecture of Mexico and Central America, as well as the tribal arts of Africa. All these elements of the past were brought into the new, future-based style.

Although Art Deco was primarily a style of decorative arts in Europe, its strongest influence in America was architectural. The ziggurat shape of many skyscrapers echoed the ancient pyramids of Mexico, while the ornamentation on the exteriors recalled stylized airliners and ocean liners. The 1930 Chrysler Building in

finding it

Since there were very few homes designed in the elaborate 1920s Art Deco style, there is obviously very little original 1920s high Art Deco hardware on the market.

It is not difficult, though, to find simple interior doorplates with hints of Deco and Streamline Moderne styling. These plates were often the only decorative touches in utilitarian homes built in the late 1930s. This hardware is found throughout the country, but most easily on the West Coast.

These later doorplates are being reproduced, as is some Art Deco furniture hardware.

practical considerations

When looking for Deco furniture hardware, make sure you know exactly what size pull you need. The center-to-center measurements vary widely.

When looking for waterfall furniture hardware, check it carefully. It breaks very easily—the plastic cracks and the pot-metal pieces snap.

If you need just one piece of waterfall hardware for a piece of furniture, be aware that waterfall hardware comes in a seemingly infinite variety of patterns and that it might be easier to find a complete set than a single piece.

decorative considerations

Later Art Deco and Streamline Moderne hardware can lend a very sophisticated feeling to almost any interior. It obviously would not harmonize with soft, floral rooms or Victorian homes, but it would be outstanding in an interior that is more modernist or industrial in flavor.

Stepped like a Mayan pyramid, the ziggurat styling of the brass lever is quintessentially Art Deco.

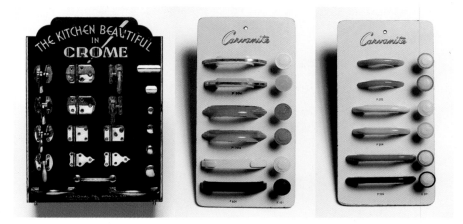

Middle America met Deco in the movie theaters and the kitchen, where chrome-plated brass and plastic cabinet hardware brought high style home.

New York is one of the most extravagant American examples of a Deco skyscraper, and the collection of buildings at Rockefeller Center (circa 1931 to 1940), with their rich interior design and monumental sculptures, is the peak of American Art Deco.

Very few domestic buildings were designed in the 1920s Art Deco style. The custom homes that were built featured brass, bronze, or nickel-plated hardware with elaborate zigzag or sunburst styling. Most American Art Deco furniture of the late 1920s was also custom-designed, with individually crafted hardware.

the streamline moderne style

In the late 1920s the Art Deco style evolved as architects and designers discovered the International style. Minimal and geometric, marked by the unheard-of use of entire glass walls supported by steel beams, this style was associated with the Bauhaus school of art and architecture in Germany. In 1931 the Museum of Modern Art presented a show entitled "International Style," featuring work from the Bauhaus.

Two years later the Nazis closed the Bauhaus, and many of its teachers and students fled to the United States. Once here, former

Bauhaus directors Walter Gropius and Ludwig Mies van der Rohe taught as well as practiced architecture, thus influencing future generations of architects. When the influence of the Bauhaus reached America, the functionalism of the International style merged with the expressiveness of Art Deco to create Streamline Moderne.

The 1934 Metropolitan Museum exhibition "Contemporary American Industrial Art" showed the full force of the Streamline Moderne aesthetic. In a domestic interior designed by architect Eliel Saarinen, industrial glass brick was used for windows for the first time, and the chairs and tables and a Steinway piano were mounted on metal legs or bases.

Furniture manufacturers quickly followed Saarinen's lead, developing spare, functional furniture made from industrial materials. A Michigan manufacturer, the Herman Miller Furniture Company, became one of the leaders in mass-produced modern furniture.

According to Herman Miller legend, one day in 1930 designer Gilbert Rohde walked unannounced into the company's offices. He could turn the flagging business around, he asserted, by designing modern furniture to replace the traditional, historical styles the company had manufactured for decades. Streamlined, utilitarian, space-saving furniture in which the design expressed the function would be the firm's salvation, he predicted.

Not only was Rohde persuasive, he was right. By 1932 he was designing all the company's modern furniture, and by his death in 1944 the company had discontinued period styles and was manufacturing only streamlined furniture, which it continues to make today.

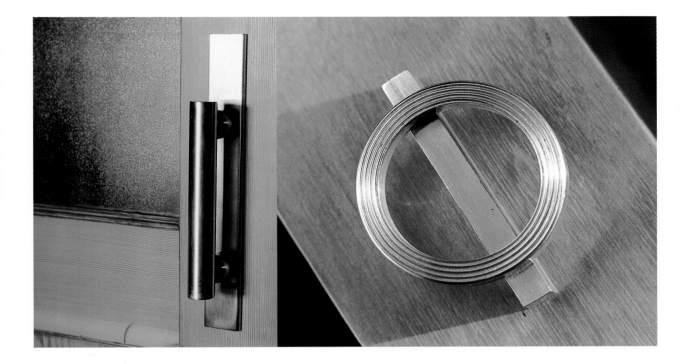

The hardware used on the modern furniture by Herman Miller and other manufacturers (including the Heywood-Wakefield Company, Karpen Brothers, and the Howell Company) looked as streamlined as the furniture. Occasionally the furniture was so streamlined that there was no hardware. Instead, cutouts integral to the piece opened drawers or doors.

The materials were also thoroughly modern—plastics like Bakelite or Lucite and materials associated with transportation and speed, such as industrial aluminum or stainless steel. When a traditional hardware material like brass was used, it was commonly chrome-plated.

Not all contemporary furniture hardware was high-end Streamline Moderne. Some of the more mainstream mass-produced furniture featured hardware that was a mixture of 1920s Deco and Streamline Moderne. Veneered waterfall furniture, which took its name from

the rounded, graduated levels of the larger pieces, was very popular during the 1930s. The hardware on this furniture is a mixture of ornamentation and materials. Curving, streamlined shapes are decorated with Art Deco ornamentation in a combination of plastic and inexpensive pot metal plated with brass.

Few pure Streamline Moderne homes were built, the monumentality of the style adapting more readily to large commercial buildings. Hardware manufacturers did produce quite a few streamlined door-hardware patterns. These pieces, usually made of wrought stainless steel or chrome-plated brass, had spare, aerodynamic lines. Exterior

More curves in a pair of mahogany beds. This style of wall sconce, a popular Deco fixture, uses slipper shades, so-called because the shade slips into the fixture.

door hardware on Streamline Moderne buildings often looks like a continuation of the building's sweeping curves.

In an attempt to thoroughly modernize door hardware, some manufacturers began experimenting with the function of the latching and locking mechanisms. Until the 1920s, a door required two knobs connected by a spindle running through a lock hand-mortised into the door. The doorknobs and the lock were different pieces, and they were sold separately.

In the 1920s, manufacturers developed cylindrical lock-sets in which the knobs and the lock are all one piece. Cylindrical lock-sets are easier to install than mortise locks, because they can be installed with a tool, not by hand. Seventy years later both types of lock-sets are still used, but cylindrical lock-sets are more common and less expensive.

The daily life of Americans—most of whom didn't own custom homes decorated with extravagant ornamental metalwork or sweeping curves—was still affected by Art Deco and Streamline Moderne. Technological advances such as cylindrical lock-sets allowed everyone to enjoy a bit of high style in their homes. Streamlined chrome and plastic drawer pulls could decorate a kitchen in any style of home, and the effect was thoroughly modern.

Earlier styles of American hardware were backward-looking, with familiar design motifs signifying stability and comfort. Art Deco and Streamline Moderne hardware was forward-looking and in motion, concerned with what was new, and what would be new. When function and modern design collided in the late 1920s and 1930s, the future of American hardware was set.

mid-century contemporary style hardware

Moderne becomes modern as America creates its own look by mixing clean lines with a stark functionalism. Refuting any historical embellishments, Mid-Century Contemporary epitomizes the innovative, no-nonsense spirit of the times. Function becomes a style all its own.

Innovations of the period include developers becoming builders and creating vast suburban subdivisions; the use of inexpensive materials like plywood, steel, and aluminum, and the widespread use of the single-story, flat-roofed house.

No-nonsense, functional, linear, and solid, Mid-Century Contemporary hardware embodied the period's optimism.

99

It's hard to remember, or imagine, how much the United States changed between 1929 and 1945. The equal of many nations at the beginning of the Depression, America emerged from the Second World War victorious, confident, supremely optimistic, and brashly assured that it had all the answers. Unfortunately what Americans didn't have were homes.

Ever so utilitarian, the aluminum doorknob and rosette are also strikingly beautiful in their simplicity.

The exterior of a 1956 tract home encapsulates mid-century style with its clean, uncluttered lines.

left: Designed in 1956 by the architectural firm Jones and Emmons for progressive developer Joseph Eichler, this kitchen takes functionalism to the logical extreme: the cabinet doors slide back and forth on runners, eliminating the need for visible hardware.

above: In a kitchen void of hardware, the aluminum switchplate becomes a built-in decorative accent.

Despite the fact that marriage and birth rates increased throughout the war, the residential construction industry had been dormant since the beginning of the Depression in 1929.

When soldiers returned to their families, they usually returned to a home or apartment housing several generations. The federal government's Servicemen's Readjustment Act, popularly known as the GI Bill, offered home-purchasing assistance for returning GIs, but there were very few homes to buy.

Original mid-century hardware is tough to find, mainly because when 1950s homes or furniture was demolished, no one thought to salvage anything. It's only within the last twenty years that this style of decorative arts has been recognized as having any merit; until then it was considered too new, too common.

There are some contemporary companies producing very simple stainless steel and aluminum door and furniture hardware that will work perfectly in homes from this period.

There are also companies making reproductions of the kitschy side of 1950s door and furniture hardware.

practical considerations

When you are able to find original mid-century hardware, check its quality carefully. There was some very long-lasting, high-quality hardware produced, but some of the period's hardware was very cheap.

If you find cylindrical lock-sets from the 1950s, make sure all the pieces are included. It's almost impossible to replace any lost parts.

Check your center-to-center measurements; the sizing on mid-century furniture handles is far from uniform.

A descendant of Eastlake and Victorian pocket door pulls, flush pulls were omnipresent on sliding closet doors in the 1950s.

Simple mid-century hardware is at home almost anywhere, in any style of contemporary interior. In fact, some of it has been continually produced for the last fifty years. Like Art Deco and Streamline Moderne hardware, it would look out of place in highly ornamented period rooms, but its simplicity works in almost any other setting.

The greatest housing boom in the history of the world was about to begin. New subdivisions proliferated on the edges of major cities. These subdivisions would be very different in both scale and style from the suburbs built before the Depression.

In the 1920s, developers had purchased areas of undeveloped land and installed streets and sewers. They then sold the land, usually block by block, to individual clients, who hired their own builder or architect, or small builders. After the war, government financing made it profitable for developers to become builders, resulting in tracts of hundreds (and later thousands) of inexpensive, virtually identical homes.

The types of houses built in the late 1940s and 1950s were also different from those built in the 1920s. Accompanied by progressive ideas about design and housing, many European émigré architects flooded the United States during and just after the war. As architecture professors, they inflamed the imaginations of young architects already buoyed by postwar optimism. These young architects eagerly pursued a brave new world. Buildings should not be clad in historical ornament, but should express their function in their materials and methods of construction.

The housing shortage of the late 1940s gave American architects an unprecedented opportunity to build houses and to demonstrate their theories about modern architecture on a wide scale. One of the most notable programs for this was the Case Study program initiated in 1945 by John Entenza, the imaginative editor of the Los Angeles–based magazine *Arts and Architecture.* Concerned that postwar architecture would pick up where it left off in 1929 and a new generation of houses would be built in Revival styles, Entenza saw the opportunity to use real houses to educate the public about modern architecture—a truly American style of architecture, a style

left: The flip side of the 1950s: kitchen kitsch. When hardware was used, it sometimes took on boisterous styling, as on these copper-tone cabinet knobs . . .

above: . . . which featured vaguely Aztec styling.

that for the first time brought the spare functionalistic aspects of the International and Moderne styles to the mass housing market.

Between 1945 and 1967 thirty-six Case Study houses were built in Southern California. Although some of the Case Study architects like Richard Neutra had flourishing practices well before the 1940s, the majority of the architects Entenza hired were young and unknown. Charles and Ray Eames were not yet world famous, and Eero Saarinen had not yet designed the TWA Terminal at Kennedy Airport in New York or Dulles Airport outside Washington, D.C.

Using inexpensive industrial materials—plywood, steel, and aluminum—the Case Study architects designed low-lying, one-story houses. Stripped of any historical references, these homes were the epitome of functionalism. The future was here, and it was no-nonsense.

Yet the future was not without beauty. Indoor atriums, floor-to-ceiling windows, and sliding doors leading to patios brought the outside in, which served to soften the hard-edged industrial tone of the homes.

The interiors utilized an open plan in which the living room, dining room, and kitchen were essentially one large room divided by groupings of furniture or counters. The bedrooms, bathrooms, and studies, placed in a separate wing, did have walls for privacy. And the automobile, that symbol of postwar optimism and prosperity, had its very own driveway that pulled up right to the front of the house.

The progressive ideas of the Case Study program were embraced by architects across the country. Philip Johnson and Mies van der Rohe each designed glass pavilions, steel-framed houses with only glass for

Sliding glass doors brought the outside in in open-plan 1950s tract homes. Manufactured by Florence Knoll, the sideboard was equally at home in dining room or office. The pulls on the sideboard are simple leather loops.

All the latest living room materials: plywood, wire, fiberglass. Designed by Charles and Ray Eames and manufactured by Herman Miller, the plywood cabinet—just like the built-in cabinets in the kitchen— has no visible hardware. Minimalism is definitely the byword.

walls. "Modern architecture" became a subject of great interest. Soon tract developers, usually motivated more by dollars than by design, were building one-story homes with flat roofs and open plans.

A particularly progressive developer in California, Joseph Eichler, hired two architectural firms, Jones and Emmons (who designed a Case Study house) and Anshen and Allen, to design homes for subdivisions in Northern and Southern California. Eichler homes are modified Case Study homes for the masses. Low-slung, one-story buildings with flat shed roofs and exposed beam ceilings, the homes feature open plans and spacious patios.

Even William Levitt, the largest residential real estate developer in the immediate postwar period, incorporated aspects of modern architecture in his huge Levittowns in Long Island, Pennsylvania, and New Jersey. Young families flocked to the developments, which each encompassed at least 15,000 inexpensive, mass-produced homes, along with community swimming pools, playgrounds, and "village greens." Levitt offered flat-roofed "contemporary" styles, but most of his homes were boxes clad in simple Cape Cod styling. He did use open-plan interiors and placed the living room at the back of the house, where it opened onto a patio.

Eventually, most developers and builders incorporated some version of modern home design into their plans. Whether nestled next to a country club or hard by a freeway, all across America homes built in the 1950s and '60s proudly featured entryways defined by half-walls, multipurpose "rumpus rooms," and sliding glass doors leading to the back patio.

These homes all incorporated very similar hardware. While the materials used in 1950s door hardware picked up where Streamline Moderne hardware left off, the shapes were even simpler. Streamline Moderne hardware had been aerodynamic, seeming to float off the door, while the aluminum and stainless steel hardware of the 1950s was solid and earthbound. Door hardware incorporated

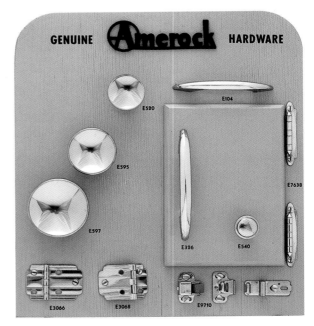

very simple forms, such as round knobs set into completely circular or square back-plates.

The furniture in a 1950s tract house was also a direct descendant of its Streamline Moderne predecessors. The ghost of the streamlined silhouettes remained, but it was slimmed down, made lighter. And new materials were exploited to their fullest capacity by large manufacturers like Herman Miller and Florence Knoll, who made furniture versatile enough to be used both in the office and at home.

Wire-frame legs made upholstered chairs and tables by Eero Saarinen easier to move around the open-plan interior. Plywood furniture by Charles and Ray Eames was even easier to move. And pieces by Harry Bertoia made only of wire or plastic were the easiest of all—they could be moved through the sliding door from living room to patio with the greatest ease.

Furniture hardware mimicked the home's structural supports. Tiny I beams marched across George Nelson desks and dressers, opening drawers. Mere slips of steel stood sentinel on Paul McCobb credenzas. Sometimes the silhouette became so sleek that hardware disappeared altogether—for instance, kitchen cabinets that slid back and forth on runners.

At the end of the decade new kitschy motifs from the Atomic Age, such as miniature Sputniks and boomerangs, began appearing on both door and furniture hardware. The optimism and confidence of the postwar era began to be tinged with misgivings about an uncertain future. For a brief period America's confidence in itself had been mirrored in the starkly functional design of its hardware. With the present beginning to turn uncertain, designers would once again look to the past for comforting reminders of a simpler time.

109
■
mid-century
contemporary
style hardware

top: 1950s styling was usually as spare as could be . . .

center: . . . but occasionally there was a hint of Deco left behind.

bottom: Found in a variety of finishes in kitchens and bathrooms across the country in the 1950s, this hardware is still being manufactured.

contemporary hardware

From the beginning of the Space Age to the new millennium, no one style has dominated. In the age of "anything goes," last year's look is this year's revival. Hardware is eclectic.

One of the most profound influences upon design since the early 1960s is the increasing shrinkage of the world. Trends and styles that once took decades to migrate around the planet now take minutes. Concurrently, what could have been "in" for as long as a hundred years now could be "out" by lunch. Gone are the times when one style could dominate. Now the byword in architecture and the decorative arts, as well as in builders' and furniture hardware, is eclectic. We live in the age of anything goes.

In the 1960s furniture hardware manufacturers began to experiment with space-age acrylics and other plastics. Art Deco styling was rediscovered (in fact, the term "Art Deco" was coined in 1966), and reproduction Deco furniture became all the rage for a while.

The 1970s saw a renewed interest in the past. Across the country, ambitious urban pioneers began reclaiming run-down Victorian and Arts and Crafts homes, painstakingly restoring these treasures. Hardware manufacturers began to capitalize on this market for period reproduction builders' and furniture hardware.

111

A clean, contemporary doorknob in brushed nickel.

The 1980s was a period of experimentation as well as reaction. A collective of Italian designers from Milan called Memphis shocked the world by using playful shapes and incongruous materials on everyday objects. High-tech designers and architects used industrial materials for everyday objects, and built buildings with all the utilities and services exposed, such as the Pompidou Center by Renzo Piano and Richard Rogers in Paris. Progressive architects like Frank Gehry deconstructed buildings, adding harsh materials like barbed wire and corrugated metal and then putting all the pieces back together in surprising, unexpected ways.

above: In a 1980s kitchen, stainless steel countertops and handles lend a high-tech, industrial feeling.

opposite: The opposite of high-tech, this kitchen blends a variety of elements from different periods into a soft, almost rustic style. The wooden cabinet knobs are purposely mismatched.

using contemporary hardware

finding it

Contemporary hardware is everywhere these days. You can find it in specialty stores, home centers, and mail-order catalogs.

practical considerations

The main consideration when purchasing contemporary door or furniture hardware is size—be sure to carry all pertinent dimensions with you.

decorative considerations

Almost anything goes with contemporary hardware.

opposite: Brightly colored, jewel-like resin knobs.

below: A riot of shapes and colors in a sitting area. The brightly colored cabinet and closet knobs echo the creative chaos.

At the same time, some American architects appropriated very traditional motifs like peaked roofs, arches, and columns, painted them pastel colors, and developed a new style called Postmodernism. Taking this concept even further into the realm of urban planning, the New Urbanism movement attempted to recapture the small-scale, mixed-use, pedestrian atmosphere of small-town America, creating communities like Seaside, Florida, from the ground up. Mediterranean motifs continued to be popular, as were those from the American Southwest. And the "country" style was a perennial favorite.

Throughout much of this explosion of styles, hardware was, for all intents and purposes, not experimental. Simple cylindrical lock-sets with undecorated knobs were installed by the millions on the doors in suburban tracts and urban town houses across the country. And in all those kitchens, very simple handles and knobs marched across the kitchen doors.

With the boom economy of the last decades of the twentieth century, hardware has seen a resurgence as an important decorative art. There are now thousands of international manufacturers producing furniture and builders' hardware in a dizzying array of styles. From the sleekest chrome handles designed by young Italian architects to handmade, hand-painted ceramic cabinet knobs, there is literally something for everyone.

Perhaps this new eclecticism is simply an updated version of older revivalist tendencies. Only time will tell. What we do know is that never before in the history of American hardware have there been so many choices for consumers to make. And just as assuredly, we also know that the next "big thing" in American hardware could be just around the corner.

part II:
inspirations,
options,
answers

inspirations,
room by room

You've now seen two hundred years of decorative American hardware, and you can tell the difference between an Eastlake drop pull and an Art Deco doorplate. But what if you don't live in a historic home? Can you still use decorative hardware if your home isn't a Victorian museum or a mecca of Spanish Colonial Revival?

Of course you can. The first thing to realize is that your possibilities are limitless. Inspiration is everywhere, and there are no rules.

As we take you on a room-by-room tour showing different ways to use hardware to express personal design styles, keep in mind the two main strengths of decorative hardware. It can be used either to blend a door or a cabinet into the overall design scheme of the room or to call attention to the door or the cabinet. Both methods are valid, and both can be used in a single room.

With the following rooms as illustrations of decorative hardware's creative potential, let your mind go. Get inspired!

entrances

The hardware on your front door is the last piece of home you touch when you leave and the first piece that greets you when you return. Front doors and their hardware are literally the divisions between the public world and your personal sanctuary. They also play an important role in welcoming your friends and family and expressing the decorative mood for the rest of the house.

In addition to covering a gamut of decorative styles, front door hardware is available in a variety of functions. The most common entrance system is a thumb-lever handle with a cylinder lock. But, as long as security issues and local building codes are addressed with an adequate lock, there's no reason not to use a decorative, oversize knob.

Decorative doorbell covers can be chosen to match almost any style of front door hardware, as can door knockers, traditionally used as decorative and functional accents to well-turned-out doors. Mail slots allow you to receive your mail without leaving the house. (Be careful, though—most antique mail slots are nowhere near large enough for modern magazines!)

opposite: A vibrant front door on a turn-of-the-century cottage boasts an iron Eastlake mail slot and a thumb-lever/cylinder lock-set circa 1920–1940. This pattern of thumb lever was used quite frequently on front doors across the country. Referring to the decoration at the top of the back-plate, which vaguely resembles an acanthus leaf, this thumb-lever pattern was called the Parthenon in the 1936 Schlage hardware company catalog.

left: An oversize knob and back-plate greet visitors with a robust sense of style.

above right: On a contemporary rendition of an Arts and Crafts home, this artful door with mortise-and-tenon joint detailing features a custom thumb-lever handle and cylinder lock. The actual handle and thumb piece are vintage pieces, while the cylinder lock is new. The back-plates were custom-made, specially designed to incorporate the handle, thumb piece, and lock into a beautifully detailed Arts and Crafts entrance system. **detail, above left:** The traditional Arts and Crafts styling of the new custom-designed back-plates blends the vintage thumb piece and handle with the new cylinder lock. The silhouette of the back-plates recalls the detailing of the woodwork in the Gamble House in Pasadena, California, the 1908 Arts and Crafts masterpiece by Charles and Henry Greene.

opposite: New and old wrought-iron hardware mix it up on the door of this Spanish Colonial Revival house built in the 1920s. The numbers and knocker are brand-new, while the grille, cylinder-lock cover, and thumb lever are original to the house. Sympathetic detailing and finishes allow all the elements, regardless of their age, to blend in beautifully. **detail, left:** This new iron door knocker is based on a design that dates back to the Middle Ages.

living rooms

Traditionally, living rooms have been the most formal room in the house. Tastes change, customs change, hemlines change, but for the most part living rooms continue to be the "dressed up" room in our homes. (At parties, all the guests may end up in the kitchen, but they usually pass through the living room first.) We put our best faces forward in our living rooms.

So living room hardware requires some strategic planning. While it may not be as obvious as your front door hardware, it still can go a long way to helping you set a design tone for your entire home.

Your options abound. If there are doors leading from the entrance hallway into the living room, think about them. Do you want them to be the same as the rest of the interior doors in the house, or do you want the living room door hardware to be unique? If it's going to be unique, how unique will it be—do you want it to relate thematically to the rest of the house's hardware while still being different, or do you want it to be in a class all its own, screaming "Look at me!"? Either approach is appropriate, but the second version takes a bit more courage.

right and overleaf: Decades and continents melt together as an American Victorian pocket doorplate joins the romance in a living room rich with the exotic sensuality of late-1930s China.

Living room windows and built-in furniture are also opportunities for creative uses of hardware. And as with the doors, you can choose hardware that will blend in with the rest of the room and house. Or you can make a bold statement with your hardware choices. It's up to you.

Freestanding pieces of furniture involve their own strategy. If you're using Great Aunt Alice's antique side tables in your living room, you probably won't want to replace their original hardware—in fact, if the tables are valuable, you'll probably decide to use them as a central component of the decorating scheme. But if you're using side tables that you found at the flea market, classic antique hardware can lend a sense of timelessness, and quirky contemporary hardware can express your individual attitude.

Whatever you decide to say with the hardware in your living room, say it confidently.

In a very contemporary Moderne living room, striking chrome-plated pulls with jewel-tone glass inserts are decorative accessories in their own right, becoming accent pieces just like the glass and ceramics. **detail, above**: The sparkling glass insert is handblown.

opposite: This 1914 Colonial Revival's brass door levers are original to the house; they work seamlessly with the living room, which—while it is elegant in a timeless way— is not a period room.

right: Flanking the entrance to an antique-filled living room, the floral and scroll forms of the Victorian doorplates are echoed in the rug. A note on authenticity: the screws in these plates are modern Phillips head screws, which didn't become popular until the twentieth century. For truly authentic applications of antique hardware, use slotted-head screws.

detail, above: In an unusual but effective pairing, a run-of-the-mill glass doorknob used in countless houses in the 1920s and '30s teams with a very ornate Victorian doorplate.

family rooms

While living rooms are decorated with an eye toward entertaining, family rooms are designed for relaxation. Whatever the name— "sitting room" in the Victorian era, "den" for Arts and Crafts advocates, "rumpus room" for 1950s tract developers—there's usually some space in every home designed solely for personal comfort. Space that might not be kept as spotless as the living room, space where putting your feet on the sofa just might not be a major transgression.

Your approach to family-room hardware will be almost the same as it was in the living room. Door and furniture hardware are the main players, and the same functional questions will arise. But since most family rooms are by their very nature less formal than living rooms, they offer a chance for playfulness, for just a bit more inventiveness in the hardware.

opposite: In a fanciful re-creation of an Edwardian gentleman naturalist's study, Eastlake walnut drop pulls— which originally graced a massive walnut armoire or dresser—seem quite at home.
detail, left: The incised brass back-plates of the drop pulls complement the rich, striated textures of the painted cabinet.

above: Hybrid styles and vibrant colors blend in a collector's den. The wooden knobs on the primitive dresser and coffee table are original to the pieces.

left: Built-in storage units in a comfortable family room feature a plain Victorian cabinet latch and bin pulls; the subdued finish of the hardware blends with the quietly sophisticated textures and hues of the rest of the room.

dining rooms

Generally, there are fewer hardware opportunities in dining rooms than in the other public rooms of a house. You've got your door and window hardware decisions, and maybe there's a freestanding or built-in serving piece that needs knobs or handles. But don't confuse fewer opportunities with limited opportunities; in fact, you can let your imagination soar with the hardware you do use. After all, dining rooms provide sustenance, and what is decorative hardware if not a functional feast for the eyes?

Used throughout the house, elegant pulls serve different purposes in different rooms. In the living room, they were accent pieces, beautiful objects blending with the other beautiful objects in the room. Here in the dining room, they help turn a cabinet, usually a quite ordinary piece of furniture, into a piece of art. **detail, left:** Elegance in glass and chrome.

above: A room's door and window hardware do not have to match. Surrounded by American primitive pieces in this sunny dining room, the hardware itself is not at all rustic, nor are the individual pieces in the same pattern. But because the doorknobs and window fasteners are subtle and unobtrusive, they add their own charm to the happy jumble of objects.

detail, left: These doorknobs were manufactured in the late 1930s and '40s. The brass center is surrounded by a hollow plastic sleeve; similar knobs utilized Bakelite sleeves.

opposite: The simple swirl on this casement fastener and casement stay has been a design motif on hardware for centuries.

bedrooms

Bedrooms are refuges. They provide shelter when we are at our most private and unguarded, and they provide security as we end one day and start the next. Bedrooms are where we dream.

They may also be where we watch television, read, work, study, and play with the kids. A bedroom is asked to fulfill a lot of requirements.

How you use the room will determine the hardware you'll use. At its most basic, bedroom hardware involves a door, a closet, and maybe a dresser. But you may need hardware for a desk, a dressing room, or an entertainment center. You may want the bedroom door hardware to be the same as the door hardware in the rest of the house, or you may want it to be different. Whether you want a very clean, contemporary bedroom, or something softer and more romantic, there's a piece of hardware for every mood.

left and below: A blend of textures and patterns gives this sophisticated bedroom the subtle sensuality of the 1940s. While from an entirely different era, the late-nineteenth-century glass cabinet knobs mingle beautifully, adding a refined feeling to the mirrored closet doors. **detail, below right:** This Victorian doorplate is used throughout the house. In the public rooms it is accompanied by an Eastlake knob; here in the bedroom, a glass knob adds a softer touch.

A tapestry of old and new in the bedroom of a mid-century tract home. Art and furniture from the 1950s blend with primitive figurines and a new custom console headboard. The handles on the drawers have been manufactured since the 1960s and for a period in the 1980s decorated almost every new kitchen built. **detail, above:** Popularly called "wire" handles (because that's what they appear to be made of), these chrome pulls do exactly what they were designed to do with quite a bit of style.

Original to the 1914 Colonial Revival house,
the glass cabinet knobs and handles in the
dressing area carry out the room's calm. They
also provide a quiet backdrop to the personal
treasures displayed in the room.

Feminine without fuss. Used throughout the house, 1940s doorknobs complement the rustic iron bedstead and grandly peeling dresser. Reproductions of furniture pulls used in France during the eighteenth century, the single-hole drop pulls on the dresser date from the 1920s, when they were widely used.

bathrooms

There are certain givens to bathroom design: a bathroom needs to be easy to clean, and it needs to function. (And there needs to be plenty of hot water, but that's not really a design issue.) Beyond that, once again, it's a matter of taste.

Do you want a rustic room? Or an ultra-contemporary one? Is your goal a showplace or a serene spa? Once you decide on a general feeling you want to impart, your hardware choices will fall into place.

In a 1950s tract home, the owners decided not to try to replicate the original bathrooms, but rather to decorate them in a sleek, contemporary style that complements the Mid-Century Contemporary look. As was the case originally, sometimes up-to-date sophistication means very little hardware: no handles, but a built-in soap dish, cup holder, and towel bar.

above: Reproduction iron hardware reinforces the rustic feeling of this richly textured bathroom.

right: Updated Arts and Crafts styling meets modern comfort in this graceful bathroom. The spa bath harmonizes with the meticulously detailed windows and cabinets, and reproduction hardware furthers the theme.

A tiny bathroom goes wild, Chinese-style. 1920s advertisements line the walls, and 1920s jadeite porcelain bathroom fixtures (so called because of their color) join the fun. The medicine chest and green porcelain sconce—a rare color for a porcelain sconce—are from the same period.

Vintage hardware on the vanity adds to the primitive look
of the bathroom. **detail, opposite:** The eyes have it
 on these incredible Eastlake bin pulls. The tiny iron latches
were originally designed to hold screen windows in place.

opposite: Successful eclecticism depends upon the harmony of the different
objects. In this bathroom, the rough-hewn tile counter, the wooden floor, the
rustic Monterey mirrors, and the opaque Bakelite pulls share an energetic
sturdiness. The Bakelite handles were manufactured in the 1930s. Notice
the handle on the medicine chest: the same color as the others, it has stripes.

above: To carry out the rough-hewn atmosphere of their 1920s home,
the owners made door handles from the same wood used for the doors.

kitchens

Kitchens are valuable. Just ask real estate professionals and interior designers, who happily tout the fact that you will almost always recoup the cost of a kitchen remodel when you sell the house. So kitchens have monetary value. They also have emotional value far beyond their role as the center of food preparation. They represent love, togetherness, and family.

It's a cliché, but like every good cliché it's based on truth: the kitchen is the heart of the household. It's a gathering place for family and close friends, and there are probably more important decisions and announcements made in kitchens than in any other room of the house. No matter how the American family changes, the kitchen is where we live.

Originally used in a bathroom, a nickel-and-glass soap dispenser circa 1920 is right at home in the riot of color and texture.

Nickel cabinet latches and green glass cabinet knobs find themselves in a whole new world. The painted moldings on the cabinets give the room an exotic Far Eastern feeling, and the American Victorian hardware fits right in. **detail, right:** Glass cabinet knobs like this one originally were used between 1890 and 1930. A round-top bolt fits in the hole through the center of the knob, and a nut on the inside of the cabinet door or drawer secures the knob.

For that reason we take special pride in our kitchens. They mean something to us. We collect things in our kitchens—cherished ceramics, family crystal, snapshots held on the refrigerator with tacky magnets—that say, This is who I am. Once we collect enough of those things, the whole kitchen begins to represent who we are.

As such, the kitchen is a terrific place to experiment with hardware. All those cabinets and drawers are a blank canvas just begging to be made into art. You can take any approach that appeals to you: The room can become an extension of a treasured collection in which you revisit a favorite period with antique or reproduction hardware. An inventive mixture of hardware can create the atmosphere of a warm family room. Or you can just use hardware you like to design a space that makes you happy as you cook.

Long cherished by the family, the 1920s Monterey desk inspired the design of the cabinetry. The cabinets were stained to match the color of the desk, and the lines of the desk are mirrored in the lines of the upper cabinets. The reproduction cabinet hardware was chosen to relate to the original Monterey hardware. **details, opposite:** The pointed-notch ends of the Monterey handle are recalled in the hinges and the back-plates of the ring pulls and the drop pulls.

opposite: An unusual entrance hints that the kitchen beyond won't be ordinary. On the Dutch door, a late-nineteenth-century glass knob opens the top section, while the bottom section is outfitted with an Eastlake doorknob that has been set into a Victorian pushplate. A different but complementary knob graces the other side of the door. The French dresser with rustic hardware carries out the farmhouse tone.

above and right: A fusion of diverse hardware characterizes this abundant family kitchen. Antique glass cabinet knobs, each with a different back-plate, march along the built-in cabinets and drawers, while contemporary handles spell out the contents of each drawer in the island. Antique drop pulls from the 1920s, a piece of Victorian furniture hardware, and a decorative Victorian keyhole cover adorn the backs of the stools.

above: Each of the glass cabinet knobs has a different back-plate.

below and previous page: You won't often find keyhole covers and furniture pulls on the backs of stools, but maybe it should be done more often—it looks great here!

opposite: One of the workhorses of the hardware world, a somewhat humble pulley gains prominence as it hoists a vintage clock above the kitchen.

The wooden cupboard with decorative Eastlake cabinet latches and bin pulls, plain porcelain knobs, and a rudimentary wooden stay carries out the comfortable pastoral mood of the adjacent dining room.

A multitude of textures: two colors of wood, granite, and stainless steel surfaces are accented by modern copper bin pulls and graceful stainless steel knobs. **detail, above:** Not only can hardware create a theme or carry out a mood, it can be sophisticated in its own right. In an elegant kitchen using a variety of materials, pulls in copper and stainless steel combine quite artfully. **detail, below:** Sometimes the simplest shapes are also the most elegant.

Large knobs ensure that
the drawer will always open,
even when your hands are
slippery from cooking!

above: Reproduction Eastlake handles give off-the-shelf kitchen cabinets an antique look.

right: A hand-forged iron lizard guards a pantry door.

so many options

You're pretty educated about hardware by now. You know your historical styles. You've seen some exciting and unexpected contemporary uses of decorative hardware. You're inspired.

Now, with the help of the following considerations, you can figure out exactly how you want to use decorative hardware to express your own style.

function

It's got to work. No matter how beautiful a window latch is, it won't open a door. If you need a door to close, do you need it to lock? Or just to latch? Are your kitchen cabinets drilled with one hole or two? Has your front door been drilled for a cylindrical lock-set? Or can you use an exterior mortise lock? All these questions can be answered by another question: Will it work? Your first consideration must be function.

Function is all-important: This Eastlake window lock won't open a door, but it will lock a double-hung window.

style

When choosing hardware, you have a lot of style options. You can use period hardware, or you can go contemporary. Your choice should harmonize with the piece of furniture or the rest of the room, but there are no hard-and-fast rules. Relax and enjoy yourself. And remember, there may be more than one right answer!

In a sunny contemporary kitchen, the existing pewter knobs—timeless and clean—work very well.

The square cutout knobs keep the silver tone while adding a new, sophisticated silhouette.

Black resin chevrons add a bit of movement to the kitchen.

Oversize copper knobs with attached back-plates look dignified without being stodgy.

The rust-colored resin wings brighten up the room and bring in a new freshness.

When you know you want to use period-style hardware, you have a choice between original antique hardware or reproduction hardware. There are advantages and disadvantages to each type.

availability

It is much easier to find matching quantities in reproduction hardware than in antique hardware. It will also be easier to find the same pattern of reproduction hardware in the future, should you need more.

There are many more patterns and styles of antique hardware than reproduction hardware. There are some very good reproductions being made, but there is not nearly as much variety.

If you need hardware right away, and have a good source, antique hardware will be your best bet. The lead time on reproduction hardware can be as long as six months.

authenticity

Antique hardware is a piece of the past. No matter how good a reproduction piece is, it is still brand-new. But, if you're involved in a restoration project and can't find enough antique hardware, it is far better to use reproduction hardware than to use brand-new hardware that is incompatible with your restoration.

If you're involved in a restoration project that falls under state or federal historic preservation statutes, check with the applicable agency to see whether there are guidelines dictating the type of

condition

Antique hardware is old and has been used. This means it will never be in brand-new condition, but for most people that's part of its charm.

By its very nature, reproduction hardware is in better shape than antique hardware. It won't need to be straightened, stripped, plated, or polished before you use it.

On the other hand, reproduction finishes are usually really shiny. If this isn't the look you're after, you can strip the protective lacquer and use a professional darkening solution to age the metal. You can reapply the lacquer to prevent further aging, or you can leave it off to encourage aging.

If you're using reproduction hardware, buy the best quality hardware you can afford. Quality varies greatly from manufacturer to manufacturer, and with hardware you really do get what you pay for. Cheaply made hardware will not stand the test of time, and an inexpensive doorknob is no bargain if you need to replace it in a few months.

installation

Most professional installers prefer to work with reproduction hardware because it is brand-new, and all the pieces are guaranteed to work.

Antique hardware does not always conform to contemporary building codes or regulations concerning access for the disabled. Check with your local authorities about these issues.

The existing Bakelite knobs and handles embody the streamlined styling of the dresser.

Same dresser, but oh those handles! The exaggerated floral knobs and handles are fighting with the simple, sweeping lines of the dresser.

From the marble top to the rich carvings to the black lacquer finish, this dresser almost screams excess. The decorative brass drop pull blends right in . . .

. . . and the rusty iron drop pull screams, "Get me out of here!" The finish is all wrong, and the style is not nearly ornate enough for the dresser.

opposite: This dresser was handmade in the 1950s. An enormous part of its charm lies in the gold-painted wooden knobs, which graduate in size with the drawers. **above:** These new ceramic knobs, based on Parisian street signs, give the dresser a different, pleasing look. The bold graphic quality of the knobs works very well against the red background. **below:** The tiny brass knobs are the same color as the original ones, but the size is all wrong. They're too small, so they get overwhelmed by the dresser. Also, they're not particularly functional—it would be difficult to open the large drawers with the small knobs.

materials

Glass, iron, plastic, brass, wood—you've got plenty of material options when choosing hardware. Traditionally, brass hardware was used for formal rooms and iron for informal ones, but these days your taste is your primary guide.

top: First manufactured in America around 1840, porcelain doorknobs are still made today. The cracking (also called crazing) happens naturally over time.

above left: The same plate, iron on the left, brass on the right, as seen from the front . . .

above right: . . . and the back. To determine if a piece is brass or iron, use a magnet. Iron will stick, brass will not.

Knobs, knobs, knobs
in Bakelite (the amber-
colored knob), plastic
(the cream-colored knob),
iron and brass.

quality

Like everything, some hardware is better quality than other. With metals, brass has traditionally been thought to be of better quality than iron, and cast metal is a higher quality than pressed. Glass is usually longer-lasting than plastic. Your choice depends upon how hardworking the application (kitchen cabinet knobs take a lot of abuse, while knobs on occasional tables rarely get used) and, again, on your taste.

far left: Heavy cast-brass doorplates.

left: Pressed brass on the left, cast brass on the right, from the front . . .

below left: . . . and the back.

If you use antique hardware, you may want to alter the finish of the piece. At the very least, you'll probably want to clean it slightly, which you can do quite easily with the finest grade steel wool and a soft cloth. If the piece is really dirty, you can use metal cleaner, the finest grade steel wool, and a soft cloth. Unlike fine antique furniture, antique hardware will not diminish in value if you clean it—that is, as long as you're just lightly cleaning it, not destroying the original finish!

If a piece is painted and you want to strip the paint, we explain how to do that in the next chapter. If the piece is painted and you want to keep the painted finish and just clean it up a bit, use very fine steel wool to smooth the flaking, rough surfaces, then clean the piece with metal cleaner and a soft cloth. If you're using painted hardware, please be aware that most older paint contains lead, which is a safety and environmental concern, particularly if you have young children who might be tempted to put a piece of hardware in their mouths.

One of the great charms of antique hardware is the variation in patina. If you're using antique hardware throughout your home, consider using the same pattern in different finishes.

If, however, you're working with a lot of antique hardware and want all the pieces to have the same finish, take them to a professional plating company. You'll have an assortment of finishes to choose from, and you'll be certain that all the pieces will match once the process is complete. Be sure to take all the pieces you need plated at the same time; like fabric dye lots, plating results will vary.

Reproduction and contemporary hardware is usually shiny, because a lacquer is used to protect the finish. If you'd like the piece to age naturally, you can either remove the lacquer yourself with a lacquer remover or take the piece to a professional plater to have the lacquer removed. If you'd like to darken a piece of really shiny brass, remove the lacquer, use a professional darkening solution on the piece, then either reapply protective lacquer or let the piece age naturally.

If you're purchasing reproduction or contemporary hardware, it's not a bad idea to purchase a few more pieces than you actually need. This way you'll have some spares on hand in case anything happens, and you won't run the risk of receiving a slightly different finish when you try to purchase an identical piece in the future.

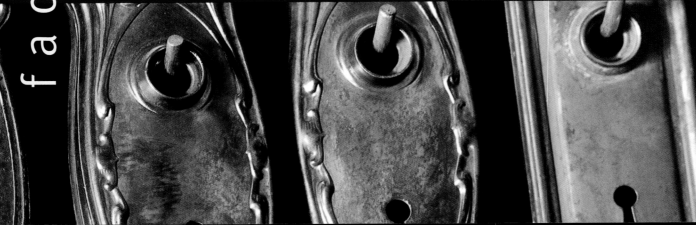

Plated, raw, painted, rusted—your finish option is determined only by your vision.

right: The same Victorian pattern, in (from the left) rust, chrome, brass, antiqued brass.

below: Six degrees of Deco (from the left): rust, japanned black (a factory finish), paint, brass, chrome, paint.

185
·
so many options

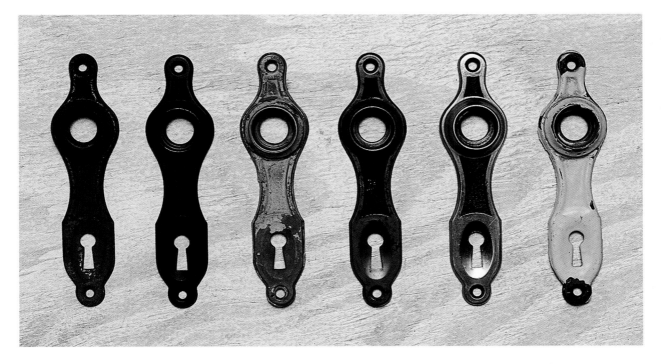

answers, and where to find them

Okay, you're ready. You've seen how other people use hardware in some pretty creative ways. You've really considered your own options, and you now know how you want to express yourself with hardware. So where on earth do you go to find the stuff?

It really depends on what you need, how many matching pieces you need, how much patience you have, and how dirty you want to get. Shopping for hardware can become a quest, or it can be just another stop in a day of errands. It's up to you.

getting some help

If you've never shopped for decorative hardware before, you're going to need some help. For this reason, we recommend that you start your search at a convenient retail hardware store. Many stores that sell the standard lines of builders' and furniture hardware also offer contemporary and reproduction hardware. These stores generally have salespeople who can answer your basic questions.

If you're not satisfied with the selection at the first store you visit, you may need to find a more specialized source. Many cities have stores that specialize in hardware—either antique or contemporary or a combination of both. These stores are your best bet in terms of both selection and customer service. Well-trained salespeople will know which questions to ask in order to steer you in the right direction, taking a lot of guesswork out of your quest for functional hundred-year-old hardware.

Another important resource these stores can offer is service referrals. Most specialized hardware dealers can tell you who to call to help with installing your hardware. This is a definite advantage if, like most people, you weren't born with a drill bit in your mouth.

opposite: A very good selection of new and reproduction builders' hardware.

left: There's a reproduction glass doorknob for any home.

Rows and rows
and rows of history:
one hundred and fifty
years of doorplates.

If you're experienced in dealing with hardware, or if you're the intrepid type who just loves getting your hands dirty and doesn't consider a job finished unless you've sweat over every small detail, then salvage yards and flea markets are the places for you.

To shop in a salvage yard, you'll need to have a pretty good idea of what you need. You'll also have to have quite a bit of patience. Most salvage yards aren't particularly well organized, and most don't specialize in hardware. If they offer hardware at all, it will most likely be a few random pieces that the owner bought as part of a larger lot. The only way you're going to know what a yard offers—used car parts or assorted pieces of hardware—is by taking reconnaissance trips. Soon you'll have your favorite yards. Be friendly—if the owner knows you're in the market for hardware, he or she can be on the lookout for it.

Finding all the vintage hardware you need to restore a ten-room Eastlake home is going to take years. Finding several mismatched pieces to accent a bathroom vanity won't take nearly as long. But going to a salvage yard is an adventure, and usually the prices can't be beat.

Salvage yards can be mesmerizing. Any good scavenger, no matter the object of desire, will feel a quickening of the pulse when confronted with a yard's hopeful beauty.

If you shop at salvage yards, you'll probably need to do some work—like stripping the old paint from a doorplate—once you get home. There are many effective strippers that advertise themselves as nontoxic on the market these days. No matter which you use, be sure to wear gloves and goggles! After you've stripped the hardware, rinse it in water, dry it, then buff it with very fine steel wool.

Painted glass, plastic, and Bakelite doorknobs should be stripped with TSP, not paint stripper. Stripper will dull or damage the finish on these materials. It takes longer for TSP to strip the paint (as much as several days, so don't lose patience), but eventually the paint will flake off the piece of hardware. Then just rinse and buff with a soft cloth.

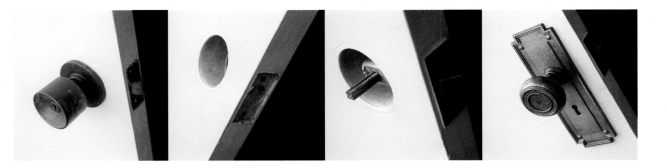

If you're intrepid, it's easy to replace boring hardware with antique hardware all by yourself. Remove the cylindrical lock-set, replace it with a tubular latch, and apply the antique doorplate (make sure it's wide enough to cover the hole, or you'll have to use wood putty around the edges of the plate) and doorknob.

Flea markets can also be great places to find hardware. The key to successful shopping at flea markets is to go early (most open at the crack of dawn) and often. If you go often enough, you can become familiar with the dealers who are most likely to carry hardware on a regular basis. If you befriend these dealers, they may begin bringing things to the market that they've picked out with you in mind. And what could be better in your search for hardware than a knowledgeable ally with contacts? Hardware at flea markets tends to be a bit more expensive than what you find in salvage yards, but bargaining is a critical part of the flea market experience. Don't be afraid to offer less than the stated price: the worst thing that can happen is that you'll be told no; usually a spirited negotiation will follow any reasonable offer.

Look carefully: hardware can be found in the most unexpected places at flea markets . . . a clown with knobs . . . a painted doorplate among crockery and glassware . . . and a collection of glass.

perfume Bottle
Circa 1870 Dug
In S.F.   DA
$45.50

talking the talk

bin pull: A cupped furniture handle mounted to the surface of the furniture.

cabinet or furniture handle: A drawer pull that requires two holes in the drawer.

cabinet or furniture knob: A drawer pull that requires one hole in the drawer.

casement stay: A mechanism used to hold casement windows open.

casement window fastener: Two pieces, a turning latch and a strike, that lock casement windows in place.

caster: A wheel that attaches to the bottom of a furniture leg.

cylinder lock: The part of a door lock, usually in an exterior application, that provides security. When a key is inserted into the cylinder lock, spring-loaded pins activate, allowing the latch to lock or release.

cylindrical lock-set: A one-piece lock- or latch-set comprised of two doorknobs and a lock or latch.

doorknob: A round or oval-shaped knob that, when turned, releases a latch.

door lever: A handle that, when turned, releases a latch.

doorplate: A plain or decorative piece placed between the doorknob or lever and the door, primarily to hold the knob or lever in place. Doorplates are often called escutcheons.

furniture rosette: A decorative piece, often circular, placed behind a cabinet knob. Also known as an escutcheon.

hinge: A jointed metal device, one leaf of which is affixed to a door rim and the other leaf of which is affixed to the doorjamb, that allows a door to open and close.

hinge pin: The pin that slides through the teeth of a hinge leaf.

keyhole cover: An ornamental metal piece, used on doors and furniture, encompassing the cutout of a key-shaped hole.

mortise lock: A square box that contains the latch mechanism to open, close, and lock a door. Mortise locks are manufactured for interior and exterior doors. Both types of mortise locks are available in a variety of functions.

pushplate: A plate affixed to the surface of an interior door, usually a swinging door, that protects the door as it is pushed open.

rim-lock: A lock mounted onto the surface of the door.

rosette: A circular doorplate. Also called an escutcheon.

sash lock: Two pieces, a lock and a strike, that join the top and bottom sashes of a double-hung window and lock the sashes together.

single-hole drop pull: A cabinet or furniture knob with a dangling ornament.

thumb-lever handle: An exterior handle with a thumb depressor that activates the latch of a mortise lock.

tubular latch: A tube-shaped lock used in place of a mortise lock.

Make sure you arm yourself with the following information before you shop for hardware. This is no time to rely on your memory.

- If you're trying to match something, you should always carry photos and a template of the piece of hardware. To make a template, lay the piece on a sheet of paper and trace around it.

- If you're not trying to match something exactly, but you have a vague idea of what you want for a certain door or piece of furniture, carry a photo of the door or the piece of furniture with you.

- If you're replacing door hardware, be sure to take the existing hardware or a photo of it with you. This will help the sales-person figure out exactly what you need.

Always carry a list of any pertinent dimensions. If you need new drawer handles and the holes are already drilled, measure the distance between the centers of the pre-drilled holes. If you're dealing with door hardware, you'll need to know the thickness of the door, the width of the stile (on a paneled door, the first panel between the side of the door and the center of the door), whether the door is solid or hollow, which side of the door needs the hinges, whether the door swings into or out of the room, and whether the door has been predrilled.

$\vdash$ — 3¾" — $\dashv$

resources

retail shops and dealers

ALABAMA

Architectural Heritage
Pepper Place
2807 Second Avenue South
Birmingham, AL 35233
(205) 322-3538
www.architecturalheritage.com

CALIFORNIA

Albion Doors & Windows
31131 Middle Ridge Road
Albion, CA 95410
(707) 937-0078
www.knobsession.com

Architectural Detail
512 S. Fair Oaks Avenue
Pasadena, CA 91105
(626) 844-6670

Architectural Salvage of San Diego
1971 India Steet
San Diego, CA 92101
(619) 696-1313

Berkeley Architectural Salvage
1167 65th Street
Oakland, CA 94608
(510) 655-2270

Crown City Hardware
1047 N. Allen Avenue
Pasadena, CA 91104
(626) 794-1188
www.crowncity.com

Liz's Antique Hardware
453 South La Brea Avenue
Los Angeles, CA 90036
(323) 939-4403
www.LAHardware.com

Manchester Sash and Door
1228 W. Manchester Avenue
Los Angeles, CA 90044
(323) 759-0344

Muff's
135 S. Glassell Street
Orange, CA 92866
(714) 997-0243

Ohmega Salvage
2407 San Pablo Avenue
Berkeley, CA 94702
(510) 843-7368
www.OhmegaSalvage.com

Santa Fe Wrecking Company
1600 S. Santa Fe Avenue
Los Angeles, CA 90021
(213) 623-3119

Scavengers Paradise
5453 Satsuma Avenue
North Hollywood, CA 91604
(323) 877-7945

COLORADO

Architectural Artifacts
2207 Larimer Street
Denver, CO 80205
(303) 292-6012

Grandpa Snazzy's Hardware
1832 S. Broadway
Denver, CO 80210
(303) 778-6508

Queen City Architectural Salvage
4750 Brighton Boulevard
Denver, CO 80216
(303) 296-0925

CONNECTICUT

United House Wrecking
535 Hope Street
Stamford, CT 06906
(203) 348-5371
www.united-antiques.com

DISTRICT OF COLUMBIA

The Brass Knob
2311 18th Street, N.W.
Washington, DC 20009
(202) 332-3370
www.TheBrassKnob.com

FLORIDA

Architectural Antiques
2500 SW 28 Lane
Coconut Grove, FL 33133
(305) 285-1330

GEORGIA

Eugenia's
5370 Peachtree Road
Chamblee, GA 30341
(800) 337-1677
www.EugeniaAntiqueHardware.com

Metropolitan Artifacts, Inc.
4783 Peachtree Road
Atlanta, GA 30341
(770) 986-0007
www.realpages.com/metroartifacts

ILLINOIS

Architectural Artifacts
4325 N. Ravenswood Avenue
Chicago, IL 60613
(773) 348-0622
www.archartifacts.com

Cavalier Antique Lighting
4412 N. Ashland Avenue
Chicago, IL 60640
(773) 728-8911

Jan's Antiques
225 N. Racine Avenue
Chicago, IL 60607
(312) 563-0275

Renovation Source
3512–14 N. Southport Avenue
Chicago, IL 60657
(773) 327-1250

Salvage One
1524 S. Sangamon Street
Chicago, IL 60608
(312) 733-0098
www.Salvageone.com

INDIANA

Colonial Architectural Antiques
5000 W. 96th Street
Indianapolis, IN 46268
(317) 873-2727

Hinges & Handles
100 Lincolnway East
Osceola, IN 46561
(219) 674-8878

LOUISIANA

The Bank
1824 Felicity Street
New Orleans, LA 70113
(504) 523-2702

Brass Menagerie
2105 Magazine Street
New Orleans, LA 70130
(504) 524-1445

MAINE

The Old House Parts Company
24 Blue Wave Mall
Kennebunk, ME 04043
(207) 985-1999
www.oldhouseparts.com

Portland Architectural Salvage
253 Congress Street
Portland, ME 04101
(207) 780-0634

MASSACHUSETTS

Restoration Resources, Inc.
31 Thayer Street
Boston, MA 02118
(617) 542-3033
www.restorationresources.com

Olde Bostonian
66 Von Hillern Street
Dorchester, MA 02125
(617) 282-9300
www.oldbostonian.com

MICHIGAN

Materials Unlimited
2 W. Michigan Avenue
Ypsilanti, MI 48197
(734) 483-6980
www.MaterialsUnlimited.com

MINNESOTA

Art & Architecture, Inc.
404 Washington Avenue North
Minneapolis, MN 55401
(612) 904-1776

Legacy Architectural Salvage
2101 Kennedy Street N. E. #190
Minneapolis, MN 55413
(612) 378-3705
www.legacy-mpls.com

MISSOURI

Bill Fellenz Architectural Artifacts
439 N. Euclid Avenue
St. Louis, MO 63108
(314) 367-0214

NEW HAMPSHIRE

Architectural Salvage
3 Mill Street
Exeter, NH 03833
(603) 773-5635

NEW JERSEY

Finishing Touches of Cape May
678 Washington Street
Cape May, NJ 08204
(609) 898-0661

Recycling the Past
381 N. Main Street
Barnegat, NJ 08005
(609) 660-9790
www.recyclingthepast.com

NEW YORK

Irreplaceable Artifacts
14 Second Avenue
New York, NY 10003
(212) 777-2900

Keystone
620 Columbia Street
Hudson, NY 12534
(518) 822-1019

Urban Archaeology
143 Franklin Street
New York, NY 10013
(212) 431-4646

Wm. J. Rigby
73 Elm Street
Cooperstown, NY 13326
(607) 547-1900

Zaborski Emporium
27 Hoffman Street
Kingston, NY 12401
(914) 338-6465

NORTH CAROLINA

By-Gone Days Antiques, Inc.
3100 South Boulevard
Charlotte, NC 28209
(704) 527-8717
www.by-gonedays.com

OHIO

B & R Architectural Salvage Company
156 Broadway Avenue
Youngstown, OH 44505
(330) 747-2907

The Brass Connection
13244 Girdled Road
Painesville, OH 44077
(440) 254-4075
By appointment only

OKLAHOMA

The Antique Hardware Store
1900 Linwood Boulevard
Oklahoma City, OK 73106
(405) 232-0759

OREGON

Aurora Mills Architectural Salvage
14971 First Street NE
Aurora, OR 97002
(503) 678-6083
www.AuroraMills.com

1874 House
8070 SE 13th Street
Portland, OR 97202
(503) 233-1874

Hippo Hardware
1040 E. Burnside Street
Portland, OR 97214
(503) 231-1444
www.HippoNet.com

Rejuvenation
1100 SE Grand Ave.
Portland, OR 97214
(503) 231-1900
www.Rejuvenation.com

PENNSYLVANIA

Architectural Antiques
3080 Bedminster Road
Bedminster, PA 18910
(215) 795-2616

Architectural Antiques Exchange
715 N. Second Street
Philadelphia, PA 19123
(215) 922-3669

Ed Donaldson
1488 York Road
Carlisle, PA 17013
(717) 249-3624
www.eddonaldson.com

RHODE ISLAND

Brassworks
379 Charles Street
Providence, RI 02904
(401) 421-5815
www.SinkLegs.com

New England Architectural Center
22 Franklin Street
Newport, RI 02840
(401) 845-9233

TEXAS

Adkins Architectural Antiques
3515 Fannin Street
Houston, TX 77004
(800) 522-6547
www.adkinsantiques.com

Architectural Warehouse
1210 Fulton Avenue
San Antonio, TX 78201

The Emporium
1800 Westheimer at Woodhead
Houston, TX 77098
(713) 528-3808
www.The-Emporium.com

The Old House Supply
1801 College Avenue
Fort Worth, TX 76110
(817) 927-8004

VERMONT

Architectural Salvage Warehouse
212 Battery Street
Burlington, VT 05401
(802) 658-5011
www.ArchitecturalSalvageVT.com

Conant Custom Brass
270 Pine Street
Burlington, VT 05401
(802) 658-4482
www.ConantCustomBrass.com

Fitz-Gerald's Antiques
48 Plank Road
Vergennes, VT 05491
(802) 877-2539

WASHINGTON

Seattle Building Salvage
202 Bell Street
Seattle, WA 98121
(206) 448-3453

WISCONSIN

Osceola Antiques
Hwy. 35, 117 Cascade Street
Osceola, WI 54020
(715) 294-2886
www.vistawave.com/antiques/

CANADA

The Old House Revival Company
782 Corydon Ave.
Winnipeg, Manitoba R3M OYI
(204) 477-4286

organizations

Antique Doorknob Collectors
of America
P.O. Box 31
Chatham, NJ 07928-0031
KnobNews@aol.com

foundations

Research and Educational Fund
of Architectural and Furniture
Hardware
c/o The California
Community Foundation
445 S. Figueroa Street, Suite 3400
Los Angeles, CA 90071-1638
(213) 413-4130

The Bosco-Milligan Foundation
P.O. Box 14157
Portland, OR 97293-0157
(503) 231-7264

museums

The Bennington Museum
West Main Street
Bennington, VT 05201
(802) 447-1571
The collection features Sandwich glass
and Bennington pottery hardware.

Lock Museum of America, Inc.
230 Main Street
Terryville, CT 06786-0104
(860) 589-6359
The collection features padlocks and
door hardware.

auction service

Web Wilson
(800) 508-0022
www.webwilson.com
Web Wilson runs periodic auctions of
antique hardware. The different lots of
hardware are illustrated on his Web
site, and bids are taken over the
telephone. He also sells antique
hardware through the Web site.

credits

We would like to thank the following for graciously providing us with incomparable locations.

HOMEOWNERS

Brian and Susan Asher; Steve Austin and Kathy Hitchcock; Karen and Frank Capillupo; Mary Beth Cornwell; Ron Crider and Jeffrey Friedman; Leah and Paul Culberg; Joan and Doug Drown; Lori Erenberg; Janna and Craig Gosselin; Ruthann and David Goularte; Virginia Kazar; Sandy Koepke; Neil Korpinen; Scott Landon; Marc Christian MacGinnis and Gregory Olton; Jim Marrin; Ruby and Ron Moore; Paul Newman; Sharon and Ozzy Osbourne; Anne and Geoffrey Palmer; Rosemary and Ralph Peters; Candra Scott; Jennifer and Evan T. Wilkes

DESIGNERS

Lori Erenberg, Lori Erenberg Designs; Ernesto Garcia Interiors; Karen Harautuneian, Hub of the House; Lisa Killian Jackson, LKJ Interiors; Sandy Koepke Interior Design; Candra Scott and Associates; Carla Smith, Hub of the House; Evan T. Wilkes, Jim Yockey, Linde Ltd.

MUSEUMS AND
OTHER HISTORIC SITES

Adamson House, Malibu, California; Banning Residence Museum, a facility of the Department of Recreation and Parks, City of Los Angeles, Wilmington, California; Craiggdorach Castle, Victoria, British Columbia; Fort Vancouver National Historic Site, National Park Service, Vancouver, Washington; Greer-Musser House, Los Angeles, California; Hale House, courtesy of the Cultural Heritage Foundation of Southern California, Inc., dba Heritage Square Museum, Los Angeles, California; The Heritage House, Port Townsend, Washington; Irving House, New Westminster, British Columbia; Oviatt Building, Los Angeles, California; Parsonage and Jason Lee House, Mission Mill Village, Salem, Oregon

RETAIL STORES

Crown City Hardware, Pasadena, California; 1874 House, Portland, Oregon; Manchester Sash and Door, Los Angeles, California

202